COURTSHIP IN CRISIS

THE CASE FOR TRADITIONAL DATING

Thomas Umstattd Jr.

To Scooter Umstattd

Thank you for sharing wisdom with your grandson
even when he was unwilling to listen.

Stone Castle Publishing
P.O. Box 5690
Austin, TX 78763
www.stonecastlepublishing.com

First Edition: August 2015

Ordering Information:
Quantity sales. Special discounts are available on quantity purchases. For details, contact the publisher at the address above.
Orders by U.S. trade bookstores and wholesalers: contact Stone Castle Publishing.
Phone: (888) 432-7734
Online: www.stonecastlepublishing.com.

TABLE OF CONTENTS

FOREWORD

By Debra K. Fileta, M.A., LPC

Once upon a time, I freaked out about dating.

I was one of those Christian singles who jumped on the bandwagon of "kissing dating goodbye"—except of course for dating Jesus.

I bought into the theory that dating was wrong and that the only way to find God's one and only match for my life would be to wait for some sort of sign from God. Wasn't that the meaning of real faith?

As an author, national speaker, and licensed professional counselor specializing in the area of relationships, I have the privilege of interacting with millions of single men and women.

As I listen to their relationship stories and look at my own relationship history, I realize that many mistakes could be avoided if we only understood that when it comes to relationships, we're often driven by fear and not by faith. Fear of abandonment, fear of rejection, fear of making a mistake, or even fear of being alone. Driven by fear, we're paralyzed in our ability to move forward.

Unfortunately, the Church at large hasn't added much to the conversation. We've created a "fear culture" around the topic of dating and relationships. We hardly talk about it, and when we do it's all fire-and-brimstone scaring us about choosing the wrong person to marry and waving the divorce rates over our heads. Besides that, our parents—the Baby Boomer generation—haven't always been ideal role models when it comes to depicting healthy, loving, committed marriages.

So, we look to the world…

There, we're bombarded by a culture that defines dating as a feel-good, romantic, emotionally driven, sexual experience. If something feels right, do it. If someone feels right, do them.

This culture embraces pleasure and passion as the foundation of relationship. Commitment is trumped by chemistry, and loyalty is replaced with lust. It's a mentality that tends to live in the moment, forsaking the building of a future.

It's no wonder that Christians freak out about dating. And it's no wonder that we're dealing with the highest numbers of single men and women we've ever had in our country. We spend years pouring fear into their lives about relationships and then wonder why so many are still single!

Rather than having the important conversations and navigating the world of dating in a healthy way, we either avoid the issue or continue to pursue relationships in an unhealthy way.

The truth is, God never intended us to live by fear. His word reminds us that "perfect love casts out fear." Not only that, but God has given us *all* the wisdom we need through His Word and by His Spirit to live by faith! Wisdom and faith always go hand-in-hand. I truly believe this applies to every part of our lives, including dating.

As I asked God for wisdom in the area of dating and relationships, I began engaging in a balancing act between the world's perspective of dating and the "Christian" perspective of dating. There is, in fact, a healthy middle ground.

I found myself empowered and my relationships enhanced. After some self-reflection, I realized that I was using dating as the scapegoat rather than addressing my baggage, my fears, and my deep-seated insecurities.

When I finally came to terms with the reality that dating wasn't the enemy, I freely addressed my own sinfulness and took accountability for my interactions with the opposite sex. I realized that I could take control of my relationships rather than allowing them to take control of me.

It's time to change the subculture we've created, which cringes in fear at the thought of interacting with the opposite sex. This book is a step toward changing this important conversation by exposing the myths and barriers that are holding us back.

Courtship in Crisis will challenge our passivity and ask us to take inventory in the role God has given us to be active participants in both our lives and in our romantic relationships. This book will challenge and teach this generation to begin living by faith and not by fear.

Singles, it's time to stop freaking out about dating and see it as an opportunity for growth, insight, and right relationships. It's time to take the pressure off "finding the one" and instead learn to glorify The One through every single interaction we have with the world around us. Dating included.

By His Grace Alone,

Debra K. Fileta, M.A., LPC
Author of *True Love Dates*
www.TrueLoveDates.com

INTRODUCTION

I grew up as a member of the homeschool community back when we still hid from the cops and got our textbooks from public school dumpsters. When I was a teenager, my friends started reading a new book called *I Kissed Dating Goodbye*. For months we talked of little else.

After reading it myself, I grew into the biggest opponent of dating you could find. I believed dating was evil, and Modern Courtship, whatever it was, was good, godly, and biblical.

My grandparents often asked why I wasn't dating. I explained what courtship was and quoted Joshua Harris, chapter and verse.

"I don't think courtship is a smart idea," my grandfather said.

"How can you tell who you want to marry if you aren't going out on dates?" my grandmother said. I tried to convince them, but to no avail. They both held the position that courtship wouldn't work.

Well, what did they know? They were public-schooled. I

ignored their advice on relationships and instead listened to the passionate, young singles around me.

As I grew older, I spoke at homeschool conferences and events. I talked with homeschool parents, students, and alumni all over the country and noticed three consistent challenges with making courtship work: identification (finding the right person), interaction (spending time with the other person), and initiation (starting the relationship).

I founded PracticalCourtship.com to encourage a national conversation to help courtship work for more people. Visits and comments poured in. Each year I waited for courtship to work for the majority of its practitioners.

It never happened.

Of the courtship community I grew up in, most members are still single. Some have grown bitter and jaded. Some of the couples who did get married through courtship have divorced.

This was *not* the deal.

Modern Courtship promised, "Modern Dating is preparation for divorce. If you follow Modern Courtship rules, God will bless you with a happy marriage." The whole point of the system was to build happy marriages, not contribute to a high divorce rate. Modern Courtship's promises weren't panning out.

I humbled myself and took my grandmother out for dinner to hear why she thought Modern Courtship was a bad idea. She had predicted its failure back in the 1990s, and I wanted to understand how and why.

What she told me blew my mind.

I met with her weekly to learn about something I've come to call "Traditional Dating." As I traveled and spoke around the country, I talked with courtship-minded singles. I told them about my grandmother's ideas. "Do you think these ideas sound crazy?"

"Actually, they make a lot of sense," many said. Several

young men who'd been burned by Modern Courtship begged me to write a post about my grandmother's observations. They wanted to try dating, but they needed someone to post a public explanation first. It took a long time to work up the nerve to tell the world I'd been wrong about Modern Courtship.

I finally wrote a blog post titled "Why Courtship is Fundamentally Flawed," which summarized my grandmother's observations. I came clean about being wrong about courtship and made a case for Traditional Dating.

> It took a long time to work up the nerve to tell the world I'd been wrong about Modern Courtship.

The post went viral.

We received over a million pageviews in less than a month. People visited from every nation (except for North Korea, but I think they block my whole blog).

Soon, readers began asking me to write a book about Traditional Dating. I didn't want to write that book, because I knew how difficult it would be. I thought writing about relationships would be like painting a giant target on my forehead. Not to mention I was still trying to wrap my own mind around these ideas.

But people kept asking. So, I decided to call their bluff. I put the book on Kickstarter and asked readers to put their money where their comments were.

It turned out they weren't bluffing.

You hold in your hands the fruit of that Kickstarter campaign. This book is the result of countless hours of work by an entire community. We went into nursing homes to do interviews, scoured scientific journals, analyzed history, and debated theology.

Hundreds of people shared their stories with me, and some of those stories appear in this book. People shared their greatest triumphs and deepest regrets. To protect their privacy and dignity, names, quotes, and identifying details have been changed.

There's nothing new in this book. As Dave Ramsey would say, "We give the same advice your grandmother would give you, only we keep our teeth in."[1] In fact, a lot of the wisdom in here came from my grandmother.

This is not a book about how to have healthy relationships. We already have *True Love Dates* and *Boundaries in Dating*, both of which are written by professional Christian counselors, offering excellent advice on how to have healthy dating relationships.

This book is a manifesto arguing for Traditional Dating as a system, model, recipe, or whatever you want to call it. It specifically pushes against the common cultural view that says, "There is no method." Most cultures throughout history have a clear system to help singles find spouses. The rejection of all systems is partly responsible for how hard it is to get married.

To keep the message clear, when I'm talking about a particular courtship system, the words will be capitalized. You can think about these competing systems as characters in a story, with Traditional Dating as the main character.

Some of the systems we will meet include:

- Modern Courtship
- Arranged Marriage
- Modern Dating
- Traditional Dating

I'm not arguing that Traditional Dating is the only method or that it will work for everyone. But I'll make a case in Chapter 7 for the benefits of Traditional Dating, in Chapter 3 I'll point out the downsides of Modern Dating, and in Chapter 4 you'll see the downsides of Modern Courtship. Then you can decide if you agree or not.

I believe Traditional Dating will help singles who follow both Modern Courtship and Modern Dating. This book is for all singles, not just conservative homeschoolers like me.

Modern Courtship claims to be the only biblical option, making all other models sinful. In this book, I present Traditional Dating as the most practical option. In other words, I won't be using the Bible as a weapon to bludgeon my opponents into silence. That said, I've done my best to keep the advice in this book in agreement with biblical principles.

My hope is that this book will remind you of a simple, flexible, time-tested recipe that you can follow to find the love of your life. The more people who practice Traditional Dating, the easier it will be to find a good match.

Quick note: You will find Q&A boxes throughout this book. You can find answers to those questions in Chapter 10.

PART 1
THE COURTSHIP CRISIS

1

THE GENERATION THAT KISSED MARRIAGE GOODBYE

A few years ago, if you had told me I'd be writing a book about Traditional Dating, I would've given you a lecture about the benefits of Modern Courtship. My parents weren't fully sold on the idea, but I suspect they were relieved when I chose not to date.

The early courtship books appealed to me. Modern Courtship felt like the safe, biblical alternative to dating. I didn't want to endure a series of heartbreaks that ultimately amounted to "preparation for divorce." I liked the idea of not giving my heart away to a woman I wouldn't marry. I wanted a lifelong happy marriage. Modern Courtship promised to be the best way to get there.

> Modern Courtship felt like the safe, biblical alternative to dating.

I didn't go on a single date in high school. When I went to college, that trend continued. I created the website PracticalCourtship.com. I wouldn't have dreamed of going on a date.

9

Looking back, I realize I'd held a deep belief that going on a date was a sin. I wouldn't have said it that way at the time, but deep down, I didn't think dating was a godly practice. The idea of going on a date terrified me.

I avoided dating. I hung out with plenty of female friends in groups, and if I really wanted to get to know a girl more, I'd create a group activity in order to spend time with her.

> I wouldn't have dreamed of going on a date.

In my early twenties, a new family came to our speech and debate club. They had a kind, compassionate, beautiful daughter who I'll call Helen. She caught my eye right away, so I volunteered to help Helen and her siblings on their speeches. I racked my brain for school-related excuses to call her.

The first time I called without an excuse, Helen stopped me. "I made an agreement with my parents that in order for a man to give me special attention, he needs to talk to my father first." I told her I understood and hung up the phone.

I knew what a meeting with her dad meant: we would start a supervised relationship for the purpose of marriage—a courtship. After no small amount of prayer and talking with my parents, I worked up the courage to call her dad and arrange a meeting.

I met her dad at a restaurant. After a bit of small talk, he drilled me with questions to determine if I was worthy. He wanted to make sure I was serious about getting to know his daughter better.

At that point, I had never been one-on-one with her and didn't know her well. But what I did know, I liked, so I assured him I was serious.

After our meeting, he told me he'd think about it, and he sent me away with some "homework," which included bringing him my résumé, a written list of life goals, and some sort of financial statement. Then he would make his determination.

I brought them.

I suffered a few sleepless nights as I waited for my second meeting with Helen's dad. When I arrived, he asked a few more questions and then said the words I'd been waiting for: "Thomas, you have permission to court my daughter. I want to continue meeting with you like this from time to time to check in on how things are going."

> "I made an agreement with my parents that in order for a man to give me special attention, he needs to talk to my father first."

A few days later, I headed off to Ecuador for a study-abroad trip with my university. (Talk about bad timing!) But we stayed in touch via email.

When I came home, I brought Helen fresh Ecuadorian roses. I handed her the bouquet, and as she smiled at me, I knew that enduring her dad's interviews was all worth it. Soon we'd experience all the happiness promised in the courtship books I'd read all those years.

Except for one problem: Helen and I didn't know each other very well. Neither of us had been in a relationship before, and we had no idea what we were doing. We just knew that whatever we did, it had to be "for the purpose of marriage."

For every five or six times I met with Helen, I had another meeting with her dad. Explaining this to my college friends proved challenging. "Let me get this straight," one of them asked during lunch. "You went on two dates with her dad before you went on a date with her?" They just didn't get it.

At first, everything about our relationship was awkward. Being near Helen was awkward. Talking was awkward.

Being identified as boyfriend and girlfriend was awkward. Despite both of us being legal "adults," neither of us had worked through the "cooties" stage of girl-guy interactions.

We weren't comfortable around each other, and we didn't know how to communicate. We felt like two kids struggling to figure out and express what we were feeling. Since I'd never been in a relationship before, I didn't know what I was looking for in a wife.

> "Let me get this straight," one of them asked during lunch. "You went on two dates with her dad before you went on a date with her?" They just didn't get it.

As you might imagine, we started having issues. I remember wondering, *Are the issues we're experiencing an indication that we're a bad fit? Or are they just things we need to work through?* I had no idea how to interpret our challenges.

We were on-again, off-again for a while, until I got word that her parents were planning to move across the country. She was living with her folks at the time and had decided to move with them.

I was devastated. I didn't want her to leave. I sought counsel from my parents and some of my courtship-minded guy friends. They thought I hadn't given the relationship enough effort, enough heart, enough commitment. I decided the best way to save the relationship was to give her a reason to stay.

So I started shopping for engagement rings.

I scheduled a meeting with her dad in order to ask for her hand in marriage. I prayed with my parents, then went to meet with her father. My insides trembled as I told him that I loved his daughter, and that I wanted to stick by her through thick and thin.

He stared at me for a moment and then said, "Thomas,

what makes you think you're good enough for my daughter?"

He went through my life piece by piece and pointed out each area where I wasn't good enough, especially in my finances.

I'd launched a tech start-up while in college. As the CEO, people depended on me for their wages. He didn't like that I wasn't working for a steady paycheck with a big company. He pointed out how my company hadn't yet taken off and that we were going through a rough patch.

His criticism didn't stop with my finances. For two hours, he methodically picked through every area of my life and explained how I fell short. Personality traits, family background, theology—very little escaped his criticism.

I sat there, too stunned to speak. None of this had come up in any of our previous meetings. In the end, he said that while he didn't think I was fit to marry his daughter, he would ask her anyway and give her the choice.

I drove to my parents' house, where I found my whole family praying for me, waiting to hear how it went. I had to tell them what Helen's father thought of me. He'd stomped on my hopes and dreams. They tried to comfort me but to no avail. I felt so numb I couldn't even cry.

My proposal to Helen came through her father, the man who'd made it clear he didn't like me. No romantic down-on-my-knees proposal for her. I have no idea what he said to Helen, but it didn't go over well.

She said no. What girl wants to be proposed to by her father?

I felt like a total failure. I worried I had sinned against God by pursuing a relationship that couldn't be from Him, since it hadn't worked out. I'd given my heart to a girl who rejected me. I was damaged goods. Who would want such a terrible person?

> What girl wants to be proposed to by her father?

#CourtshipInCrisis

That year was one of the lowest points in my life. Not only did I have to deal with Helen's rejection and her father's stabbing criticisms, but around that same time my dad had a heart attack, my grandfather died, and my business continued to lose money.

During that time, I came to the conclusion that Helen's dad must've been right. I wasn't worthy of courting Helen, much less any other girl.

I decided I would prove to him, myself, and the world that I wasn't a failure. Over the next few years, I dove into work until it consumed all my free time. I took little to no salary. I poured all the profits back into my company to get more growth. We couldn't grow big enough or fast enough for my tastes. I had to prove that man wrong, whatever the cost.

For a while, we hired a new person every month. But no matter how fast the company grew, it never felt big enough to prove I was worthy.

My parents encouraged me to go on dates. At this point, it had been years since the rejection, and they'd grown concerned about me.

A couple of years later, I met a girl through a nonprofit I volunteered for. We hit it off, and I did something I'd never done before: I asked her out to dinner. She didn't come from a courtship culture, so I didn't need to ask her dad first.

It was a pretty normal date. (Except for the fondue. I think most people stopped eating that a long time ago.) I picked her up. We shared pleasant conversation at the restaurant. I paid, and then I drove her home. I don't think I touched her once (even to shake hands or give her a side-hug).

Nevertheless, the next day guilt swirled in my heart. I'd done something I promised I would never do. I went on a date with a girl, alone, at a restaurant. We didn't even have a chaperone!

Though my parents had encouraged me to date after the

Helen breakup, I still felt that dating was evil. Had I sinned against God?

Not Uncommon

One of the aspects of my job is that I travel and speak at conferences around the world. Some of the events are specifically for the homeschool community. This gave me a chance to speak with a lot of courtship-minded folks.

I heard stories similar to mine. It turned out my experience was more common than I had thought. I spoke with one godly and ambitious young man who'd been rejected by over two dozen fathers and was still single. Most young men give up after far fewer rejections.

Some women might question whether these types of courtship-minded men really exist, but they do. I've met them. They're smart, funny, and would make amazing husbands and fathers. Yet they share Modern Courtship horror stories similar to or worse than mine.

Young courtship-minded women are frustrated that "no one is asking." They cry themselves to sleep at night because they feel alone and unwanted. They have no idea how many young men give up on Modern Courtship after suffering rejections by courtship fathers.

But when godly young men give up on Modern Courtship, it creates a gender imbalance in the community. The more people I interviewed, the more I suspected something was wrong nationwide. The imbalance is so strong in some communities that some women get the impression that there are hardly any godly men left.

> Modern Courtship promised to help us guard our hearts from the heartbreak of dating. Instead, it amplified the pain of rejection.

Modern Courtship promised to help us guard our hearts

from the heartbreak of dating. Instead, it amplified the pain of rejection.

These young men and women want to honor God. They also want to get married. Yet there seems to be no clear path from single-and-lonely to married-and-happy.

As I heard these stories, I reconsidered views from people like my grandparents, who had been against Modern Courtship from the beginning. Could their concerns have been valid? How could I have been so wrong?

I spent serious time praying and seeking God. I studied history, searching for answers. Why were God-fearing men being so cruelly rejected? Why were godly women crying themselves to sleep out of loneliness and despair? Why were there so many lonely, sad singles in the Church making comments like, "There aren't any good men out there," or "No girls ever say yes to a date"?

I was seeing a national trend that went beyond Modern Courtship and even beyond the walls of the Church.

In many ways, homeschoolers think of themselves as countercultural. But in terms of relationships, we were super-cultural. We forged ahead of culture when it came to group dating. You could almost say those of us in the courtship community were the hipsters of relationships—we abandoned dating before it was cool. Now, even on college campuses, dating of all kinds is on the decline as singles swipe right to hook up with strangers.

The courtship crisis is not hitting only conservative, courtship-minded singles, but it's also hitting people throughout our society. Each year a smaller percentage of people get married than the year before.[1]

This is a crisis many don't realize is happening, but it's one that could have long-term implications for both our personal lives and our entire civilization.

> **Q&A #1**
> I'm 25 years old, and I've never been asked out on a date. I want to get married. What should I do?

The Marriage Crisis

In the time between when my grandmother sat in that soda shop with her Friday-night date in 1946 and when I asked Helen to consider a relationship in 2008, the yearly wedding rate in the United States dropped from 16.8 weddings to only 7.2 weddings per thousand people.[2]

Since then, the marriage rate has fallen further still—to only 6.8 weddings per thousand people.[3] And some of those weddings are second or third marriages. The wedding rate in America is now at an all-time low and continues to fall. In 1946 a typical church of 300 people would have had five weddings in one year. That same church in 2014 would host only two weddings.

When people think about the "Marriage Crisis," they usually think about America's staggering divorce rates. The problem is bigger than that. While the Baby Boomer generation had trouble staying married, many Millennials won't get married at all.

In 1950, married couples occupied four out of five households. Today, for the first time in history, less than half of U.S. households are occupied by a married couple.[4] The drop in married households is particularly notable because all the "adults who still live with their parents" count as "living in a household with a married couple."

Millennials are kissing marriage goodbye like no other generation. Today, just 20 percent of adults aged eighteen to twenty-nine are married. That's down from 59 percent in 1960.[5] So in a youth group of twenty young people, only four of them will be married by the time they turn twenty-nine. The other sixteen students will have to wait into their thirties and beyond.

> In 1946 a typical church of 300 people would have had five weddings in one year. That same church in 2014 would host only two weddings.

The Pew Research center predicts that one out of four Millennials will never get married.[6] So for five of the singles in that youth group, true love will wait a lifetime only to find nothing but platitudes from well-meaning married couples. We have one generation that won't stay married and another that won't get married.

The courtship crisis isn't just a crisis of Modern Courtship. It's a crisis of all systems of courtship, both secular and religious.

Young people, parents, and churches are desperate to do something about the courtship crisis. Unfortunately, as we'll soon see, the proposed solutions didn't work, and in some cases they made the crisis even worse.

Civilization Without Marriage

You may be asking, "Why should we care about the marriage crisis? I mean, as long as you find a spouse, who cares what everyone else is doing? Live and let live, right?"

Wrong.

Marriage is the core of a family. According to Aristotle, the family is the foundation for civilization[7]. When a foundation cracks in one place, it creates a ripple of problems throughout the entire structure. Modern social science shows that when the institution of marriage cracks, a ripple of problems is caused throughout society.

For example, children who grow up *without* married parents do worse in school,[8] make less money,[9] pay less in taxes, are more likely to commit crimes[10] and require more government assistance.[11] Right now, less than half of all children are growing up in a traditional family.[12]

> We have one generation that won't stay married and another that won't get married.

But this isn't just about children. Singleness has health consequences for adults.

Unmarried people:

- are less happy[13]
- live shorter lives[14]
- have more heart attacks[15]
- are less likely to survive cancer[16]
- are more likely to get Alzheimer's[17]
- experience more depression[18]
- experience more stress[19]

If a virus causing these symptoms were to spread around the nation, we'd call it an "epidemic" and mobilize society to address the disease. People would be dumping buckets of ice water on their heads to raise awareness. When people talk about the "singleness epidemic," it's not just hyperbole. There are real physical and emotional symptoms.

The human body is only as healthy as the health of its trillions of cells. A sickness in one cell does little harm, but when enough cells get sick, the whole body will die.

A civilization, likewise, is only as healthy as the individuals who make up the society. A rise in singleness makes more adults and children sick emotionally, physically, and financially. Could anything else be as harmful to our society as the decline in marriage? Western Civilization has collapsed before, with the fall of the Roman Empire. We should beware the hubris that says it can't happen again.

> Right now, less than half of all children are growing up in a traditional family.[12]

If we don't restore the institution of marriage, we'll face a future of lonely singles left wondering what happened and who will take care of them in their old age.

The good news is that this is a problem we can fix. It's not too late for any of us. Yes, it'll take some hard work and a shift in thinking, but solving the courtship crisis is easier than you might think.

2

FROM BRIDE-PRICES TO BUNDLING BOARDS: A 4000-YEAR HISTORY OF COURTSHIP

Conservatives tend to think, *Back in the day, people were more holy*. But Scripture tells a different story. Solomon tells us, "History merely repeats itself. It has all been done before. Nothing under the sun is truly new" (Ecclesiastes 1:9). According to the apostle Paul, "The temptations in your life are no different from what others experience" (1 Corinthians 10:13a).

This means history is a lot more valuable than you might think. The generations that have come before us faced the same temptations and challenges we face today. As such, we can learn from their victories and mistakes.

People assume that by adopting Modern Courtship, they're adopting a traditional value system, and in doing so, they're getting back to the "good old days." But is Modern Courtship really a traditional system? Or is it something that cherry-picks customs from the past, the way someone would select food at a buffet? If you look at the history of dating, marriage, and courtship, an interesting story emerges.

If you find history boring, you can skip this chapter. I

don't mind. Not everyone likes history as much as I do. But if you choose to read this chapter, I suspect you'll be surprised by what you find.

Biblical Courtship: Bride-Prices and Arranged Marriages

In biblical times, men traded their daughters in exchange for a bride-price paid or for a service rendered.

For instance:

- Caleb gave his daughter to Othniel (Joshua 15:16–19) as a reward for capturing a city.
- David's first wife came in exchange for a bride price of one hundred Philistine foreskins (1 Samuel 18:25–27).
- Abraham sent his servant with ten camels' worth of treasure to buy his son a wife from Laban and Bethuel (Genesis 24:4–10, 29, 50–51).
- Jacob bought his wife from the same Laban in exchange for seven years work (Genesis 29:15–18). It seems that Laban was the "wife mart" of the ancient world.

In those days, many covenants weren't considered binding without the shedding of blood. For most covenants, animal blood would be used. You see the shedding of blood in many of the covenants that God makes throughout the Old Testament. A remnant of this kind of covenant lives on today when people cut their thumbs to become "blood brothers."

The covenant of marriage was sealed in blood as well. What made a woman married was not a legal contract or a ceremony with a priest, but rather the shedding of the woman's virginal blood. The legal proof of a marriage was the blood on the bedspread. There are examples in the Old Testament where the bloody bedsheets were admissible in court as evidence of the marriage's validity (Deuteronomy 22:13–19).

> What made a woman married was not a legal contract or a ceremony with a priest, but rather the shedding of the woman's virginal blood.

This helps explain some of the curious practices in the Old Testament.

For example, the punishment for a man who slept with an unbetrothed woman was marriage without the possibility of divorce (Deuteronomy 22:28–29), because the only person who could legally marry the woman was the man who shed her blood. He also had to pay a sizable bride-price to her father. This explains why women like Tamar, who were raped and didn't marry the rapist, didn't remarry anyone (2 Samuel 13:20).

Multiple women could shed blood to enter a marriage with one man. But a woman couldn't shed blood multiple times to enter a marriage with multiple men.

A childless widow couldn't remarry just anyone. She was supposed to marry a close relative of her first husband. What's more, her second marriage didn't have the same legal weight as the first marriage. Her first son with her second husband legally became the son of her first husband, with whom she'd shed her blood, and not the second husband, the biological father (Deuteronomy 25:5–6).

This explains why Ruth was an unattractive prospect. Ruth's first son would legally belong to her first husband's bloodline. If she had only one son, all her second husband's assets would go to another man's "son." This may also explain why Abigail's son Daniel wasn't considered in line for the throne, despite being one of David's oldest sons (2 Samuel 3:2–5). No one wanted the legal son of the unpopular and foolish Nabal to rule.

The Bible gives a few instances of women choosing their husbands and not being given or sold in marriage. For example, the daughters of Zelophehad marry *whoever they wanted* within their tribe (Numbers 36:6).

Before you freak out, I don't think these examples from Scripture are prescriptive. Just because the Bible describes something doesn't mean we should do the same. Many of the stories in the Old Testament are examples of what *not* to do. God uses broken people, and the men and women in the Old Testament were no exception.

Many of the families we see in the Bible are unhappy or dysfunctional. Sarah demands that her husband have sex with her servant (Genesis 16:1-5). Both Leah and Rachel do the same (Genesis 30:1–13).

In 1 Samuel, we see Elkanah's wife, Peninnah, making life miserable for his other wife Hannah (1 Samuel 1:6–8). Hannah suffers for years and the family never truly gets past this rivalry. It's in this story that we get perhaps the most flagrant line of masculine cluelessness in the Bible. Hannah's husband asks her, "'Why aren't you eating? Why be downhearted just because you have no children? You have me—isn't that better than having ten sons?'" (1 Samuel 1:8).

> Just because the Bible describes something doesn't mean we should do the same. Many of the stories in the Old Testament are examples of what *not* to do.

The laws regarding bride-prices and the importance of virginal blood were intended to govern the cultural practices of the time. It's God's desire that every tribe and language-group worship Him (Revelation 7:9). This vision can't be achieved if all people abandon their culture and adopt the language and cultural practices of the ancient Hebrews.

The Old Testament laws give us a glimpse into God's heart, but we must be careful to interpret them correctly today. A law forbidding the mistreatment of slaves doesn't mean God approves of slavery.

God met the children of Israel where they were and adapted laws to their culture and condition. Jesus even made a point to clarify that the Old Testament marriage laws weren't God's ideal but were instituted due to the hardness of the people's hearts (Matthew 19:8).

Classical Roman Courtship

The Romans held a different view of marriage from the Hebrews. Unlike the Israelites, the Romans were monogamous. A man could be married to only one woman at a time and vice versa.

While in biblical times the groom bought the bride from her father, in Classical Roman times the bride's father paid the groom a dowry. Roman women held their own separate property and were often entitled to keep their dowries in the case of a divorce. Roman men would sometimes need to borrow money from their wives.

For the Romans, the shedding of blood didn't consummate a marriage, but rather a contract and/or ceremony did. The early Romans held marriage in such high esteem that they killed their king and created a republic because the king's son Sextus forced a Roman woman named Lucretia to commit adultery.[1]

Later, during the decadence of the late republic and empire, the Roman view of marriage declined. After a while, the Romans swapped spouses like geeks swap comic books.

Interestingly, at about this time, Rome began its long, slow decline.

For example, Octavian forced Scribonia, the wife of Scipio, to get a divorce and marry him. He later changed his name to Caesar Augustus. The purpose of the marriage was to cement a political alliance. When the alliance was no longer needed, he divorced her.

> While in biblical times the groom bought the bride from her father, in Classical Roman times the bride's father paid the groom a dowry.

Many of our marriage practices and terms come from the Romans. The words "matrimony," "nuptials," and "divorce," for example, all have Latin roots.

Medieval Courtship

The early church rejected the Romans' declining view of marriage. The New Testament spoke highly of sexual purity and the sanctity of marriage (1 Thessalonians 4:1–12, 1 Corinthians 7). Early Christians saw marriage as a life-long commitment and even as a holy sacrament. They saw marriage as a picture of the mystery that is Christ and His Church (Ephesians 5:21–33). So priests, rather than civil officials, performed wedding ceremonies within a church building.

The early church believed that the covenant of marriage was consummated through sexual relations between the bride and groom.

This led to some awkward situations when the marriage carried political importance. For example, when the marriage sealed a treaty between kingdoms, sometimes an audience stood in the bedroom during the marriage consummation to confirm its legally binding status. Marrying Prince Charming had its drawbacks back in the day.

Since a contract or a ceremony wasn't what made the marriage binding, if the couple didn't sexually consummate the marriage, it could be annulled. So while the medieval church didn't allow divorce, it did allow annulment, which said, "The marriage never actually began."

Marriages were often arranged among the aristocracy. In fact, for royalty, marriage was sometimes forced. A family that stood to gain from an alliance could force a prince to marry whichever bride would bring the kingdom the most power. So, *being* Prince Charming had drawbacks too.

> The early church rejected the Romans' declining view of marriage.

Forced Marriage was somewhat uncommon outside the highest levels of society. In Arranged Marriage, both the bride and groom had the chance to say no. There's a precedent of this choice going back to biblical times. For example, Laban asked Rebekah if she would go with Abraham's servant (Genesis 24:57).

The poor typically had more choice than the rich. Marriage was a necessity of life since it took a family to fully work a farm. The husband provided protection, the wife provided children, and together with the children they worked to provide for the family.

While the wealthy sometimes needed permission from the king to marry, all the poor had to do was live together, sleep together, and refer to each other as husband and wife. Sometimes a priest performed the wedding ceremony years later. This ancient practice still exists in the English Common Law, forming the root of what we call a "common-law marriage."

Enlightened Courtship

During the Enlightenment, thinkers like John Locke shifted the landscape for courtship, marriage, and family. In Locke's essay *Two Treatises of Government*, he redefined family government, demolished many of the theological underpinnings for patriarchy, and made a case for individual liberty under God.[2]

America was founded on the ideas of Enlightenment thinkers like Locke. For instance, *Two Treatises of Government* directly influenced the famous phrase "life, liberty, and the pursuit of happiness" in the Declaration of Independence. Because of this, America is unique in the western world in that it has no clear tradition of Arranged Marriage.

Despite the tradition of individual liberty, until the late 1700s marriage was still seen as more of a contract than a love story. Men and women chose each other as a means to get something they needed, such as wealth or support. It's not that married couples didn't love each other before this time. But love was seen as something that would grow out of the marriage, rather than the marriage growing out of love.

> America is unique in the western world in that it has no clear tradition of Arranged Marriage.

Arranged Marriage, on the other hand, teaches that though we don't choose our siblings or parents, we learn to love them. Therefore, the same must hold true for marriage. Just because a man doesn't choose his wife doesn't mean he can't learn to love her.

The old playground singsong "First comes love, then comes marriage, then comes a baby in a baby carriage" would've been considered a revolutionary battle cry in the days of Arranged Marriage.

Enlightened Courtship taught that you'd have a happier marriage if love came first. To help love come first, people spent more time getting to know each other before marriage.

In Ellen Rothman's book *Hands and Hearts: A History of Courtship in America*, she points out that "parents exercised little control over their children's courtships."[3] Young people spent a lot of time together unsupervised by adults. "In the half-century after Independence, middle-class youths expected and experienced considerable autonomy in courtship."[4]

Rotherman goes on to say, "By the end of the eighteenth century 'the way and custome of the country' was to leave marriage making to young people."[5] When parents did influence the decision it was, "more in the matter of *when than of whome* their children would marry" [emphasis original].

> Love was seen as something that would grow out of the marriage, rather than the marriage growing out of love.

The early Americans experimented with new courtship practices like bundling. Inspired by the story of Ruth and Boaz, bundling allowed two single people to sleep together in the same bed. One or both of them would be sewn up in separate "bundling bags," sometimes also separated by a "bundling board." You can see this portrayed in the movie *The Patriot*, starring Mel Gibson.

You have to wonder how effective those bundling bags were, since as many as one out of three brides were pregnant at their weddings in the late 1700s.[6]

In the early 1800s, people began to seek relationships passionately and emotionally instead of analytically.[7] The tension between these two contrasting views of romance is captured in some of Jane Austen's books.

While the Victorian era saw a high-water mark for outward displays of chastity, parents weren't as involved then as they are today, and the rates of premarital pregnancy dropped during the Victorian era.[8] Parents in those days took a more hands-off approach to parenting.

The fictional account in *Tom Sawyer* does a good job of capturing a glimpse into nineteenth-century small-town culture. The book contains a story in which school-aged children couple up and go into a cave unsupervised with only candles for light. Could you imagine parents allowing their children to do something like that today?

Other novels that capture this hands-off parenting approach are *Little Women* and the *Little House on the Prairie* books.

Twentieth-Century Courtship

By the early twentieth century, more marriages sprouted from love than for mutual material benefit. Some pockets of aristocratic culture still practiced Arranged Marriage, but most of the Western world, and specifically American culture, married for love.

Bundling was mostly abandoned (though some Amish communities still practice it today) as young people used more modern ways to get to know each other. Community dances served as a key part of the courtship process in the late nineteenth and twentieth centuries. The dance allowed young singles to interact with many other singles in one night.

> The early Americans experimented with new courtship practices like bundling.

In some ways, the community dance has a lot in common with the modern practice of speed dating, with a five-minute song keeping time rather than a facilitator with a bell. Young men who came to a dance alone would offer to walk one of the young women home (think *It's a Wonderful Life*). This could result in long moonlit chats on many a front porch.

Both men and women looked at dating as an essential step toward their future happiness. They went on dates to intentionally get to know each other and to have fun. They dated to find their perfect match.

By the mid-1950s, the cultural standard was that young men "earned the right" to go steady by going on dates with lots of different women. Both men and women intentionally pursued each other romantically.

What those dates looked like varied from community to community and from couple to couple. They may have gone out somewhere in town, and they could have even stayed home with their families. But even at home, they were afforded some measure of privacy so they could really get to know each other.[9]

> Young people in junior high were encouraged to spend time together one-on-one but were discouraged from "going steady."

There was a distinction in those days between "dating" and "going steady." Young people in junior high were encouraged to spend time together one-on-one but were discouraged from "going steady." These non-exclusive, platonic dates gave young people a chance to get comfortable with being one-on-one with the opposite sex. The dates also gave them a good understanding of what kind of person would make a good match.

There's a modern assumption that parents in this time period were very involved in their children's romances. I couldn't find much evidence of this in the literature of the time, so I asked my grandmother what her parents told her about dating.

From what I can tell, they hardly ever talked about it. The

only thing they told her was, "Don't go steady, don't have sex, and be home by ten." They also wanted to know if the young man came from a "good family," but their involvement didn't go much beyond that.

This hands-off style of parenting may sound crazy in a day where helicopter parenting is the norm. But the shift to micromanaged parenting is so modern that it happened in my own lifetime.

I remember playing in the street with the other children from the neighborhood. As I grew up, more and more parents moved childhood play from the neighborhood to the back yard. Play has since moved from the back yard to the living room PlayStation.

University of Georgia professor Richard Mullendore blames the rise of the cell phone for the explosion of helicopter parenting. He calls cell phones "the world's longest umbilical cord."[10]

Traditionally, parents allowed their children to roam freely for long periods of time and over large areas of town. This expanded as children learned to ride a bicycle. Children could make their own decisions and mistakes. You can even find vestiges of this "bicycle freedom" in old episodes of *Adventures in Odyssey*.

Parents often explained that the rise in crime justified the shift to close supervision. But in reality, the crime rates have been dropping to historic lows.[11] What is rising is fear.

People in the 1950s feared the consequences of physical relationships. They wanted that sexual relationship, but they also wanted to wait and "do it right." No one wanted a premarital pregnancy. In Traditional Dating, first came love, then marriage, then the baby.

They maintained a cultural standard for purity, but this standard was often enforced by each person's conscience rather than strict parental supervision.[12] If a couple got pregnant, they were punished with a "Shotgun Wedding" where the community forced them, sometimes with actual shotguns, to get married.

If we had frozen time in the 1950s, our modern perspective on dating and courtship would be different. Young people would frequently go on dates, not to be promiscuous, but because they wanted to find what kind of person would make a good match.

But time didn't freeze. Instead, our culture shifted once again.

3

WHY MODERN DATING IS FUNDAMENTALLY FLAWED

Recently, on the radio, we talked about how one problem with Modern Courtship is that you can put a comma after any sentence that has to do with courtship and add "for the purpose of marriage." This adds an awkward additional meaning to common phrases.

For instance:

- "Could I get your phone number, *for the purpose of marriage*?"
- "Would you like to get coffee, *for the purpose of marriage*?"
- "I'd like to get to know you better, *for the purpose of marriage*."

Those five words—"for the purpose of marriage"—put undue pressure on budding relationships and make it harder for true love to develop. A young man is unlikely to ask a young woman to coffee when that invitation is tantamount to a marriage proposal.

With Modern Dating, on the other hand, you can put a comma after any sentence and add, "for the purpose of sex."

For instance:

- "Could I get your phone number, *for the purpose of sex?*"
- "Can I take you out to dinner, *for the purpose of sex?*"
- "I bought you these flowers, *for the purpose of sex.*"

> A young man is unlikely to ask a young woman to coffee when that invitation is tantamount to a marriage proposal.

And these five words are *even more destructive* than their Modern Courtship counterpart. In today's culture, "for the purpose of sex" dating has become the norm for many singles. It's the seawater that most fish swim in. While many accept this new "Modern Dating" as normal, those of us in the Christian community don't accept it as a healthy or normal practice. We don't think Modern Dating leads to strong marriages or happy lives.

As I talk with people about Traditional Dating around the country, some folks think I'm crazy. "It's inconceivable that you'd recommend dating in our sex-saturated culture," they say.

The confusion comes from the word "dating." In response, part of me wants to wield my best Inigo Montoya accent and say, "You keep using that word. I do not think it means what you think it means." Just because *some* water is salty doesn't mean *all* water is salty.

To understand the difference between Modern Dating

and Traditional Dating, we need to look at where Modern Dating came from.

Modern Dating & the Sexual Revolution

In the early twentieth century, society tended to look the other way if the couple had sex before marriage, as long as they got married afterward. The threat of a "shotgun wedding" kept most couples on the straight and narrow.

Then came "the pill."

Effective birth control masked the evidence of sexual activity. Many Baby Boomers rejected the "because I said so" values of their parents and started sleeping around. This Sexual Revolution began in the 1960s and brought several new societal ideas about sex and marriage.[1]

As Boomers introduced sex into dating relationships, those relationships changed. Sex brought with it emotional bonds, intensity, and drama. It also brought an expectation of faithfulness. A man could "cheat" on his girlfriend by sleeping with another woman. This wasn't adultery. No marriage vow had been broken, but it violated the new cultural expectation of faithfulness between unmarried sexual partners.

About this time, the language for relationships shifted. What was once called "going steady" came to be called "dating." Instead of saying, "Bob and Jean are going steady," Baby Boomers would say, "Bob and Jean are dating." What was once called "dating" soon became "dating around" and "playing the field." Both were considered derogatory terms.

> "It's inconceivable that you'd recommend dating in our sex-saturated culture," they say.

Instead of going out with different people on platonic,

low-commitment dates, Boomers skipped Traditional Dating altogether and went steady right away.

Dating, something that was once fun, safe, and effective, transformed into a series of heartbreaking relationships. Each decade following the Sexual Revolution intensified the sexual element of dating. What started off as just a "hippie thing" entered the mainstream in the 1970s and 1980s.

> Dating, something that was once fun, safe, and effective, transformed into a series of heartbreaking relationships.

Typically, someone would go on one, two, or maybe three dates, and then they expected to "go steady." By the 2000s, group dating grew in popularity, allowing singles to jump right into "going steady" without going on a single "date" first. By 2004, one in three American singles were having sex on a first date.[2]

For many singles, saying yes to a date means saying yes to sex, which makes the date a bigger deal and a bigger commitment. The idea of dating many different people in order to find the right one morphed from a way to find a good match into a way to catch a sexually transmitted disease.

The Sexual Revolution created something few wanted or expected. Adding sex to dating made relationships more exclusive, committed, and intense. It also led to heartbreak after heartbreak.

Modern Dating Is Less Romantic

In Modern Dating, there's little incentive for men to woo and pursue a woman beyond the first few dates. In response, women who follow Modern Dating often complain about the lack of good men. But once a man gets a woman he hardly knows into bed, what incentive does he have to continue to fight for her heart? This lack of pursuit is what leads to the apparent lack of good men.

Let me explain. There's an unwritten "bro code" that most men follow. I'm not sure where it came from, but if you don't believe me, ask one of the guys in your life.

Some tenets of the bro code include:

- Don't take the urinal next to another bro, unless there are no other options.
- Don't hold hands with another man.
- Don't go after another guy's girl.

Once a woman is going steady, no guy will pursue her unless he's willing to break the bro code. The kind of men who break the code are generally not the kind of men most women would want as a husband.

As soon as two people become "an item," the bro code prevents competition from most other men. In Modern Dating, women are either isolated by the bro code or available to be "claimed." Once a woman is "claimed," the bro code kicks in, so there's little competition for her.

> If you're a woman and you want men to treat you with respect, Modern Dating is not for you.

This lack of competition allows men in Modern Dating to treat women poorly since they then have little competition from other men. If you're a woman and you want men to treat you with respect, Modern Dating is not for you.

In Traditional Dating, on the other hand, couples don't go steady right away. This season where men compete for women's hearts trains men to treat women with respect. These honorable habits can last a lifetime. Men want what other men want, so if a man is interested in you, it'll make you more attractive to other men.

In these situations, the bro code says, "May the best man win." So in Traditional Dating, the bro code pushes men to be the best men they can be to win the woman's heart.

For example, when my sister started Traditional Dating last year, she got a lot more attention from the men already in her life. They sent flowers to her office, took her to nice restaurants, and planned fun dates because they wanted to woo her. They knew they were in competition with other men who were also asking her out.

> In Traditional Dating, the man has to fight for the woman's heart. This fight forces him to be both honorable and intentional.

In Modern Courtship, on the other hand, the man has to ask the father for the woman's heart. The father gives his daughter to the man, and it's *the father's* heart that must be won—not very romantic. I can hear the courtship pickup lines now— "Hey girl. Your dad wants us to be together."

In Traditional Dating, the man has to fight for the woman's heart. This fight forces him to be both honorable and intentional. Competition spurs men toward excellence. A man who knows his date is being pursued by other men is less likely to take her to the local Greasy Spoon and more likely to bring flowers.

Modern Dating Makes Couples Too Close Too Fast

Courtney loved Edward. She loved his big brown eyes, his perfect smile, the way he made her feel like the most beautiful girl in school. She was certain they would marry when they got older, so what did it matter if they had a bit of fun?

What harm could it do? Courtney was only sixteen when she had sex with Edward on a band trip.

When Edward broke up with her during her first semester of college, she was devastated. She couldn't leave her dorm for days. She finally convinced herself that sex was just a physical act. It didn't mean anything, and neither did Edward.

As if to prove this to herself, she began to sleep around. She didn't lack for guys at college who wanted to sleep with her. At first the attention felt great, but after a while the "just a physical act" made her feel sick inside. She wanted someone to love her as a person and not just see her body as a means to an end.

As a senior in college, she started going back to church. At first, she feared that once they knew about her past, they'd ridicule her. Instead, she found the love of Christ in the people at her small group. A few months after graduation, she finally surrendered and put Christ back on the throne of her life.

A few years later, she met a young man named Ricardo on the worship team, and they decided to get married. But even then, the pain of her sexual past led to deep struggles with their sex life. Only after many more years of counseling did she work through the wounds that came from assuming sex was merely a physical act.

Modern Dating tells singles like Courtney that sex won't affect their emotional and spiritual well-being. It says that hooking up is fun. It says that sex is safe if you use a condom.

Once the hook is set, couples are robbed of the joy that comes from intimacy *with* commitment. Modern Dating leaves singles feeling vulnerable, alone, and heartbroken when their too-close-too-fast relationships disintegrate.

#CourtshipInCrisis

Oxytocin—An Unhealthy Shortcut to Love

In the last few years, scientists have discovered a lot about what goes on in the brain during sex. I imagine those were some fairly awkward studies to conduct. Fortunately, we can learn the results of those studies without going into all the details.

When a woman has sex, her brain floods with oxytocin and some dopamine. Oxytocin is called "the bonding hormone" because it leads to greater levels of empathy, attachment, and trust.[3]

When a man has sex, his brain gets flooded with dopamine and a little oxytocin. Dopamine fires the pleasure center of the brain.

This hormonal asymmetry leads women to typically have more feelings of love and trust after sex than men. While men are more likely to get addicted to the sexual act itself, women are more likely to get addicted to the man. This is a neurochemical explanation for why some women find it hard to leave an abusive man.[4]

Oxytocin creates strong emotional bonds in both men and women. It causes a woman to feel a level of trust and affection for a man, even if he has done nothing to earn it. This emotional shortcut reduces the need for him to woo her in the future.

Third-Degree Heartbreak

When I was a kid, I helped clear brush on my grandparents' ranch. We gathered the brush into a big heap and then set it on fire. When we ran out of lighter fluid, we started the fires with gasoline.

Gasoline burns so hot and fast that it often burned away before the brush caught fire. Temptation followed, and we threw more gasoline on the embers to rekindle the fire. Cupfuls of gasoline created mushroom clouds and heat but produced little fire.

Gasoline burns so aggressively that fire can climb up the liquid and into the container where it then explodes. A friend of my dad's once got third-degree burns all over his body doing this.

When I joined the Boy Scouts, I learned a better way to start a fire. The key to building a big fire is to start with a tiny fire and then grow it over time. If you start small enough, all you need is one match.

No gasoline needed. No third-degree burns.

Adding sex to a dating relationship is like pouring gasoline onto a fire. It makes everything more intense, but it doesn't make the relationship healthier.

In Modern Dating, physical intimacy comes before compatibility and far before commitment. This means that the inevitable breakup hurts far more than it would have without a physical relationship. Creating and severing those heart ties again and again carves emotional scars that can last a lifetime.

Modern Dating Reduces the Incentive to Marry

I interviewed a man named Geoffrey, who said that when he was younger, he didn't want to get married. His parents' divorce was so painful that he didn't want to risk experiencing the same pain. Divorce burned him, and he didn't want to touch that hot stove again. When he married, he wanted it to be for life.

Years later, after he moved in with his girlfriend Kristen, he still didn't want to get married. But his reasoning had changed. He said marriage was "just a piece of paper. We don't need the government to say what we have is real."

Why the huge mindset shift?

Modern Dating asks, "Why buy the cow when you can have the milk for free?" This kind of thinking is disrespectful to women. Even the metaphor is offensive. For Modern Dating, sex is the motivation, and if someone can get that without marriage, why get married?

Once Geoffrey slept with his girlfriend, he subconsciously moved her from the "potential wife" category to the "free milk" category. Some women think that if they sleep with a man it will convince him to tie the knot, but that's not how men typically think. So that plan may backfire. Men have an aversion to committing to women who are easy to sleep with. For more about the science behind this, read Duana Welch's fascinating book *Love Factually*.

If Kristen wants Geoffrey to marry her, she'd be wise to say no to sex until Geoffrey says "I do" to lifelong commitment. With Modern Dating reducing the incentive to marry, is it any wonder that its rise corresponds with a rise of singleness?

Modern Dating Is Preparation for Abuse & Divorce

Modern Dating claims that cohabitating before marriage increases the chance of marital success. But is this true?

To answer this question, the National Institute of Mental Health commissioned a study from a research team at the University of Denver.[5] This team looked over dozens of scientific studies about cohabitation. The results of the research were clear.

Couples who cohabitate before marriage have:

- poorer communication
- lower marital satisfaction
- higher levels of domestic violence
- greater probability for divorce.

Any one of those outcomes makes for a solid reason to avoid cohabitation, but all together they swirl into a toxic cocktail of marital misery.

But could this be correlation instead of causation? The researchers looked into that question too. They controlled for religiosity, education, income, and other variables, and they found that the results persisted. There was a causal connection between cohabitation and more miserable marriages.

To explain why, the researchers shared a story about Rob & Emily.

The Slow Slide into Marital Misery

Rob and Emily meet at a party where they exchange numbers. They text a few times and decide to go to dinner. Dinner leads to drinks, and drinks lead to Emily sleeping over. She sleeps over again a few nights later. After a while, Emily buys a toothbrush to leave at Rob's place. Then a hairbrush.

Rob gives her a key, and pretty soon she has a drawer in his dresser and stays there two or three nights a week. Then four or five nights a week. Soon they begin to wonder, "Why are we paying rent for two apartments?"

So she moves in. After a fight about money, they sign a one-year lease to share the rent.

But Emily starts to wonder if Rob really is the man she wants to spend her life with. She thinks about leaving, but breaking the lease would be too expensive. He's not "that bad," so she sticks around. Staying is easier than leaving.

Then Emily gets pregnant. They decide to get married. They

wake up together and drive to the wedding. After the honeymoon, they go back to the bed they've shared for so long.

A year later, Rob lies in bed wondering if he would have married Emily if they hadn't lived together first. Did he make a bad choice? He feels frustrated and stuck with Emily.

His frustration leads to an argument and soon plates and dishes are hurled back and forth across the apartment. Finally, to protect the baby from a toxic home environment, Emily flees to a women's shelter and later files for divorce.

> Modern Dating's promise that living together first will lead to a happier marriage is a lie.

The Cohabitation Effect

Would Emily and Rob have gotten married if they hadn't lived together first? In each of these steps they slid into the next stage of the relationship instead of stopping to consider if it was a good idea.

Were they a good match? How would they know, since for most of their relationship they felt stuck with each other? Living together cheapened the wedding, turning it from an event where lives were changed to a ceremony that celebrated the way things already were.

When a friend asked Rob how they ended up living together, he responded that it "just happened." Each step felt like the easiest option at the time. The longer they stayed together, the harder it was to break up. They slid into marriage and later slid into divorce. No intentional or prayerful decision. No pursuit. No romance. Just a long, slow slide into marital misery.

Modern Dating's promise that living together first will lead to a happier marriage is a lie. There have been dozens of studies on this in multiple countries, and they all come to the conclusion that cohabitation leads to more divorce. The science is clear that cohabitation leads to situations that are bad for men and even worse for women. Less deliberation leads to poor matches and less marital satisfaction.

Not to mention that living together cheapens the wedding, when the wedding merely states that they are living together.

Modern Dating—The Wrong Recipe

Imagine a mom who wants to teach her young son how to bake cookies.

First she pulls out an old recipe card she received from her mother. She patiently walks her son through the instructions. They add butter, sugar, flour, chocolate chips, then bake the cookies in a 350-degree oven for ten minutes. The cookies come out of the oven to cool. Then they dunk them in milk and eat them. Delicious.

Can you imagine how it would go if she simply told her son to head to the kitchen and follow his heart?

"There is no one recipe for cookies," she tells him. "Everyone makes cookies differently, so just do what seems best to you."

I can picture it now. This boy with no experience in the kitchen pours cups of sugar over a sprinkling of flour. Soon, blobs of dough sit for hours in a 500-degree oven. Finally, the fire department shows up to handle the aftermath.

If you have no experience baking, you need a recipe. Just because there are multiple recipes for cookies doesn't mean that all recipes are worthless. I've tried quite a few "healthy" cookies that I'd gladly never try again. Some recipes are better than others.

The thinking in America is that since there's no one way to find a spouse, there should be no recipe at all. Young people with no relationship experience are expected to figure it out themselves. This thinking is a recipe for failure.

> Adding sex to dating is like putting ketchup on cookies. They aren't good together.

Modern Dating added sex to the recipe. It seemed like a good idea at the time. Sex is fun. Dating is fun. Two fun things together must be double the fun. Right? Wrong.

Adding sex to dating is like putting ketchup on cookies. They aren't good together.

It's time to go back to grandmother's recipe card.

But first, let's look at one more experimental recipe that our culture tried in the 1990s.

4

WHY MODERN COURTSHIP IS FUNDAMENTALLY FLAWED

By the 1990s, Baby Boomer conservatives had grown frustrated with the promiscuous nature of Modern Dating. They didn't want their children to repeat the mistakes of the Sexual Revolution. Parents became more involved in their children's love lives and in some cases took it over entirely.[1]

Conservative leaders like Bill Gothard, Douglas Wilson, and Jonathan Lindvall formulized a new set of rules that they called "courtship."[2] These rules blended the values of Arranged Marriage, some practices of Modern Dating, and some practices of Victorian Courtship (but without the bundling bags).

Before this time, "courtship" meant any process of getting married. Scientists even use it to describe the practices of some animal species.[3]

The best-selling Star Wars book *The Courtship of Princess Leia* came out in 1994, followed by *Her Hand in Marriage: Biblical Courtship in the Modern World* in 1997. I like to think Star Wars helped popularize the word "courtship" before conservatives started using it, but that's probably wishful thinking.

Modern Courtship hit the mainstream with Joshua Harris's book *Boy Meets Girl: Say Hello to Courtship*. By the late 1990s, even people in the secular world had grown disillusioned with how broken Modern Dating had become, and courtship-related books flew off the shelves.

Modern Courtship attempted to address the problems of Modern Dating, but instead of arguing that we go back to the less-committed relationships of Traditional Dating, it argued that relationships should become even *more* committed. Instead of my grandmother's "don't-go-steady rule," Modern Courtship mandated, "Get her father's permission first, because this relationship is for the purpose of marriage."

> **Q&A #2**
> Is Joshua Harris to blame for the courtship crisis?

In this way, Modern Courtship exacerbated the too-close-too-soon problem that started during the Sexual Revolution. The promise of less heartbreak in courtship is sadly unfulfillable unless you marry the first person you court. Otherwise, Modern Courtship can prove just as heartbreaking as Modern Dating.

The implementation of Modern Courtship spurred a drop in the marriage rates among Christian young people. Each year, fewer Christian singles were getting married. The Church inadvertently walked hand-in-hand with the world in abandoning marriage.

A Modern Courtship

Jennifer was the quintessential stay-at-home daughter. She even ran a blog advocating the stay-at-home-daughter lifestyle. She spent her days encouraging women to stay at home and devote themselves to their fathers while learning valuable homemaking skills. On top of encouraging women, Jennifer waited patiently for her dad to approve a good match for her.

After years of waiting patiently, he said yes to one of the men who asked his permission to pursue her. Jennifer's gut told her almost immediately that it might not be a good match, but her church and her father told her it was, so she plodded on.

One Sunday after church, they went on a "date" to Burger King. He didn't buy Jennifer any food. They just sat there talking and not eating. "It was just so awkward," she said. She wanted to call it off then and there, but her family pressured her to stay in the relationship.

As she went out with him, he became controlling and manipulative. Yet she stayed because she didn't want to be "damaged goods" for going through a failed courtship. She did her best to trust her church and her father in finding her a suitor, all the while wondering why it felt so wrong.

A few months later, he asked her to marry him. She felt flattered to be asked and said yes. Her friends were so excited that they couldn't sit still. Jennifer was one of the first women in her church to get engaged in a long time. It was all anyone could talk about for weeks.

> **Q&A #3**
> I courted and I am now happily married. How can you say it doesn't work?

Everyone was excited. Everyone except Jennifer. She sat there in the eye of her own internal storm, wondering about the disquiet in her heart about this man.

After the engagement, they were allowed to hold hands. "He wouldn't let go of my hand. It was like a leash. If I wanted to scratch my arm, he'd be upset," she said. "I felt trapped and scared. He just got more and more controlling about little things in my life."

Jennifer did her best to submit to his demands, but as she did, she wondered if his level of control was really abuse. *If engagement made him worse, will marriage make him even worse still?* she asked herself in her darker moments. Her church taught total female submission, so she did her best to follow those teachings even though she lived in a constant state of stress and fear.

> **Q&A #4**
> I courted, and now I am in an abusive relationship. What should I do?

Finally, she realized that she was afraid to be around him. She dreaded their time together. So she prayerfully came to the conclusion that she had to break off the engagement. Before she could talk to her fiancé, she had to first sit down with her parents and explain why things weren't working out. After that meeting, she wrote a letter and read it to her fiancé about why she had to call off the courtship.

After the breakup, she began to study Scripture and allow God to shape her own personal beliefs. She realized that Courtship as her church taught it wasn't in the Bible. This led to a conversation with her parents in which she told them she could no longer be a stay-at-home daughter. Instead, if she was going to continue living with them, she would have to have some autonomy as an adult.

Her parents were shocked. They spent hours trying to convince her otherwise. But Jennifer held fast. She stopped allowing rules to lead her and instead, turned to her Creator.

She sought counseling to help her work through the abuse she'd suffered in her engagement.

When I talked with Jennifer, I applauded her for her bravery. I've heard from many young women in her position who went on to marry abusive men that their fathers had approved. Many of them either lived in constant fear of their husbands or filed for divorce and fled their communities.

What Is Courtship, Anyway?

After twenty years of conversation, there's still no consensus as to exactly what "courtship" is. The more I speak with courtship-minded Christians around the country, the more definitions and practices I find.

When I write about courtship online, defining courtship often becomes *the most controversial* point in the comments. I believe that the lack of a clear definition may be contributing to the crisis.

Each community feels that its form of courtship is superior to the others. Many feel that any problem pointed out in Modern Courtship as a whole doesn't apply to them because their flavor of courtship is superior. This inconsistency feeds the courtship controversy.

Instead of addressing courtship as a whole, I'd like to discuss each component individually. That way, if your community doesn't follow one of these aspects of courtship, you can just skip that section.

Modern Courtship Is Exclusive

In Modern Courtship you can court only one other person. Going out with different people one-on-one in order to get to know them is forbidden.

Once someone enters an exclusive courtship relationship, they're tempted to feel that "this is my only chance. If this fails I'll be *damaged goods*, and no one will want me." The early exclusivity and commitment can lead to giving your heart fully to someone you may not yet know. Entrusting your heart too early to someone you barely know can lead to painful heartbreak. Modern Courtship promised we wouldn't experience heartbreak if we avoided dating.

If only that were true.

Some of the people most passionately against courtship are those who spent years piecing themselves back together after a "failed courtship."

Courtship, for the Purpose of Marriage

Remember how I said in Chapter 3 that most courtship activities could include the phrase "for the purpose of marriage" after them? It's one of the most common courtship tenets.

This kind of thinking leads to unintended consequences. Offering to take a girl out for ice cream is tantamount to asking for her hand in marriage. Awkward! That's why men hesitate to ask, and women are reluctant to say yes. Making each interaction "for the purpose of marriage" makes relationships too serious too soon.

I talked with a young woman the other day who complained, "No guys are asking me out." I reminded her that one of my friends had asked her out just a few weeks before. She replied, "Yes, but I don't know if I like him. I can't go out with someone when I'm unsure how I feel about him." If my grandmother were there, she would say, "But how can you know if you like the guy if you won't go out with him?"

> Making each interaction "for the purpose of marriage" makes relationships too serious too soon.

You can't really get to know someone if you only interact with him or her in a group setting and through private text messages. There has to be actual face-to-face interaction.

Courtship Requires Parental Approval

Mark adored this girl named Emma. He eventually asked Emma's roommate to jot down Emma's father's number when she wasn't looking. That way he could call Emma's dad.

He called, asked for a meeting, and then drove to her hometown early on Saturday morning to meet her dad at a coffee shop. They had met before, but nothing compared to this meeting where he would ask that life-changing question.

> **Q&A #5**
> Why can't we just spend time in groups?

His hands trembled as he gripped the steering wheel. Every red light lasted an eternity. He felt fairly certain Emma's father would say yes to courtship, but he really wanted to honor her and her family by asking her father's permission. He loved Emma so much, and he didn't want anything to stand in the way of their Happily Ever After. So much was riding on this conversation.

What both Mark and Emma's father didn't know was that Emma didn't like Mark. She secretly hoped Mark would just leave her alone.

Mark did his best to convince Emma's father that he was a good man. It seemed a bit like talking with a banker, trying to get a loan approval. Mark succeeded and won Emma's father's heart. He had no idea how to win Emma's heart or even that he needed to try. The months that followed were painful and awkward for all involved.

According to *Her Hand in Marriage* by Douglas Wilson, one of the first Modern Courtship books, "A *date* is when a young man and woman go out together on their own, and *courtship* is when a young man goes through the young woman's father."[4] The book goes on to say, "The authority of the father extends over the romantic interests of his daughter."[5]

Wilson makes a special point to explain that this is true even for adult daughters.

In forms of courtship that require parental approval, the man must fight for the father's heart, not the woman's heart. If this sounds unromantic, that's by design. As Douglas Wilson says, "This whole area of men and women coming together has been a propaganda playground for modern sentimentalism."[6]

The one area where Wilson breaks from the Old Testament practice is that he doesn't advocate, to my knowledge, that a father should receive financial compensation for giving his daughter in marriage.

The point when a man needs to obtain parental permission varies from community to community. In some communities the man needs permission before he can spend time one-on-one with the woman, while in others permission isn't needed until they want to "become a couple." Some families even require young men to go through an extensive interview process where he submits anything from signed statements of faith and purity vows to tax returns and résumés.

> Parents in Traditional Dating see themselves as coaches rather than kings.

Because of this, courtship fathers typically hold a "permission and control" role rather than the "advice and blessing" role that their fathers held before them. In patriarchal families, this "permission and control" continues into the adulthood of daughters and sometimes for sons as well.

This is a problem because it either goes too far or not far enough.

Modern Courtship gives parents the right to veto any relationship. In essence, they have only a very definitive no vote. The more people in the relationship with a no button in front of them, the higher the likelihood one of them will press it. The result is that fewer people get married. In this way, courtship goes too far.

Compare this to Arranged Marriages where parents have both a yes and a no vote on the relationship. This method results in more marriages because parents may also say yes. In this way, Modern Courtship doesn't go far enough. If you trust your parents to say no for you, then why wouldn't you also trust them to also say yes for you?

In Traditional Dating, the single person has both the no and yes vote. Parents are consulted, and the more they are trusted, the more their advice is heeded.

After all, it's the singles who will marry and stay together for the rest of their lives, not the parents. So the singles should be the ones making

> The more committed the couple, the easier indiscretions are to justify.

the decision. Parents in Traditional Dating see themselves as coaches rather than kings.

Courtship Requires High Accountability

Courtship *needs* high accountability to function because of how committed the relationships are.

Let me explain. No, there is too much. Let me sum up.[7] When are you more tempted to compromise sexually? Is it on the first awkward date when you're so nervous you can't eat, or three weeks before the wedding? Most people would answer "three weeks before the wedding." Temptation increases with commitment.

The more committed the couple, the easier indiscretions are to justify. And when you know you're going to marry the person before you've even had a cup of coffee, it's pretty hard to flee temptation.

"We're going to be married soon anyway," the engaged couple says, justifying their actions.

The problem with courtship is that by making things "for the purpose of marriage" right from the beginning, you have near-engagement levels of temptation from the beginning. That's why younger siblings watch courtship couples like a hawk and why some parents demand to read each text message.

The courtship trend of high accountability at the beginning of the relationship and lower accountability as the couple moves toward marriage is exactly backward. First dates are awkward enough without a third wheel sitting there not talking—or worse, not shutting up.

Let me be clear: accountability is a good thing!

Everyone should have friends and mentors who hold them accountable. We all need someone to challenge and encourage us. But the girl's father serving as the accountability partner for the young man isn't healthy accountability. It's awkward accountability.

> **Q&A #6**
> Are you saying parents should be uninvolved in the process like they are in Modern Dating?

The father has a conflict of interest when it comes to holding the boyfriend accountable. He loves his daughter. He doesn't love the man the same way, if he cares at all. His love for his daughter motivates him rather than his love for the man. Accountability without love can be toxic.

If the relationship doesn't work out, the young man needs someone to sit with while he cries into his ~~beer~~ iced tea. That's not going to be the father of the girl who just broke his heart.

This kind of paternal accountability often represents the

form of accountability without its function. Imagine a young man frustrated about the relationship or who is tempted sexually. Would he call the father of the woman for advice and encouragement? Most men would skip that accountability session, and where does that lead them? More temptation and less accountability.

Courtship Comes Packed with Purity Rules

Each courtship community maintains its own rules about physical contact and purity. Some communities forbid kissing until the wedding day. Others allow kissing after the engagement. But most courtship communities agree on the need for strict purity rules.

The courtship culture and the purity culture swim in the same pool. Or rather, they would swim in the same pool if that were allowed.

> Accountability without love can be toxic.

One man, Phillip, told me, "I was determined to keep a standard of purity. I did this because I wanted to honor God, but also because I wanted to honor my future wife. Courtship seemed like the perfect solution to help me hold to that standard. If we followed the rules, it would be nearly impossible to slip up!"

"The problem," he said, "was that we were so accountable, we never had a moment to get to know each other. Sure, we didn't have physical temptation, but we also didn't have quality social interaction. After we got married, I felt like I'd married a stranger."

Marrying someone you realize you don't know sounds pretty scary. If you're going to walk down that road, why not go all the way and embrace an Arranged Marriage?

When I graduated from high school in 2004, a family friend gave me a CD set of the NIV Bible. (This was back in the days when we had to put little plastic discs into a slot in our cars to listen to something.) After a few years, I made it to the book of Galatians. I listened to it over and over. It took months, but Galatians reprogrammed my mind.

> Depending on purity rules to keep you pure is like depending on the Law to make you righteous.

I realized that trying to trust God *and* trust the rules wasn't the Gospel. I started to believe deep down that the Christian walk wasn't about following the rules.

Following Jesus means the Spirit of Christ lives in our hearts and directs our lives.

Purity is important, but rules don't make us pure. Human accountability is no replacement for the Holy Spirit in our hearts, leading us in the path of righteousness.

> Yet we know that a person is made right with God by faith in Jesus Christ, not by obeying the law. And we have believed in Christ Jesus, so that we might be made right with God because of our faith in Christ, not because we have obeyed the law. For no one will ever be made right with God by obeying the law.
>
> Galatians 2:16

Depending on purity rules to keep us pure is like depending on the Law to make us righteous. It didn't work in the days of the apostle Paul, and it won't work today.

Does this mean I'm saying we're free to sin? Absolutely not! The Holy Spirit won't lead us into sin. But it's Christ's Spirit in us that makes us pure, not us following human purity rules. If Jesus is Lord of your heart, you don't need rules. If He isn't Lord, no amount of rules can save you.

If you grew up in a community whose leaders focused on following the rules, I encourage you to do what I did. Read the book of Galatians and see what Paul has to say about such leaders. Read it in different translations and let the truth really seep in. "So Christ has truly set us free. Now make sure that you stay free, and don't get tied up again in slavery to the law" (Galatians 5:1).

> Purity is important, but rules don't make us pure.

The law is like the moon: It's not a source of light. It's only a reflection of the light. The moon is much smaller than the sun, yet if it gets in the way, it can block the sun's light and cast the world into darkness.

Purity rules can become so important that we lose sight of The Light that is The Spirit of Christ living in us. Don't let purity rules cast your life into darkness. It's a miserable way to live.

Courtship Is Intentional and Intense

Modern Courtship discourages long relationships and long engagements. The "for the purpose of marriage" intensity is so high that shortening the relationship feels like the best way to prevent compromise.

But cutting the relationship short may not be best for the couple. It takes time to get to know someone. When you rush the relationship, you can go so fast that you don't discover the other person's true self until it's too late.

I've received multiple comments from young women who had no idea how abusive and controlling their boyfriends were, because they didn't have enough time to get to know them. When they did spend time together, the girl's father supervised and the man stayed on his best behavior.

One young woman commented on my blog, "In my case,

I wasn't allowed enough face-to-face time with my suitor and then fiancé for me to get to know him properly before making (what I assumed was) a lifetime commitment to him. I've often wondered—if I'd gotten to know him well enough, would I have picked up on the fact that he was a closeted gay?"

When I talk with Baby Boomers, they often don't understand why relationships are so awkward for us Millennials. So for the Boomers reading this book, find a young person and ask them, "Is Modern Courtship awkward?" You may be surprised at how passionately they say, "Yes!"

> **Q&A #7**
> What do you think about secret courtships?

Greater intensity leads to greater awkwardness. There is a lot to be said for slowing down and reducing the intensity.

Courtship Requires Marital Readiness

Modern Courtship teaches that you shouldn't enter into a relationship until you're "ready to get married." This sounds like good advice. Who wants to get married when they're not ready? The problem is that this advice is completely unbiblical.

We live in a sex-saturated culture. The Bible doesn't tell us to wait out temptation; it says to flee temptation (1 Corinthians 6:18; 2 Timothy 2:22). If we can't leave our culture, what should we do? The good news is that when we are tempted, God always gives us a path of escape (1 Corinthians 10:13), and the biblical escape for the temptation of lust isn't a cold shower—it's marriage. Glorious, sexy, messy marriage. Paul told us to marry lest we burn with lust (1 Corinthians 7:9).

I suspect God knew we'd be tempted to procrastinate marriage, so he put frequent encouragements in the Bible for us to marry *young*.

The Psalmist says, "Children born to a *young* man are like arrows in a warrior's hands" (Psalm 127:4, emphasis added). Solomon says to "rejoice in the wife of your *youth*" (Proverbs 5:18, emphasis added).

Here's what the Bible doesn't say: "Children born to the *ready* are like arrows in a warrior's hands." It does not say, "Rejoice in your wife once you are *ready*." Could we have made readiness into an idol?

The trend in America is to put off marriage for financial reasons, only to later spend tens of thousands of dollars on fertility treatments because the couple waited so long to get married. This trend is only good for people selling fertility treatments.

Some people delay marriage for emotional reasons. They push aside great matches to wait for that perfect soul mate. They ignore that years of singleness can create singleness issues that they will bring into a marriage. The only way to attract a perfect person is to be a perfect person. I could be wrong, but I think that's impossible. This means the only people left on this planet have flaws.

I suspect, when people put off marriage until they have the perfect job, a full bank account, and a fancy house, they do so out of fear. My parents' fondest memories are of their time together as poor married students. They still talk about the time when my dad looked in the pantry and there was nothing but pancake mix, sauerkraut, and syrup. Not dissuaded, he combined it all into what made for a terrible meal but a wonderful memory.

> If money can't make you happy, can it really make your marriage happy?

If money can't make you happy, can it really make your marriage happy?

Can someone ever really be ready for marriage? I don't know a single married couple who, when looking back, says they were really ready. Typically, they describe marriage like jumping off a cliff into a cold lake. They thought they were ready, but when they hit the water, the cold and excitement knocked their breath away.

Marital readiness is like a carrot on a stick, which a donkey keeps trying to bite, but can never quite reach. This leads to frustration for young people and an unnecessarily long time to withstand temptation.

> Modern Courtship is not in the Bible. Calling it "biblical dating" doesn't make it biblical.

It should be no surprise to see that very few singles can withstand this temptation indefinitely. They weren't made to. They were made to rejoice in the husband or wife of their *youth*. As Solomon says,

"Farmers who wait for perfect weather never plant. If they watch every cloud, they never harvest." (Ecclesiastes 11:4)

But Wait, Isn't Courtship Biblical?

The most ardent criticisms of my blog came from those who assume that Modern Courtship is biblical. One woman told me, "Courtship was almost a basic tenet of faith in my church as I was growing up. The Bible tells you to court with the permission of your parents. I was shocked when I read about the issue in the Bible myself and found just the opposite."

Like I said in Chapter 1, for years I also felt Modern Courtship was "the holy way," and dating was "evil." Once

I dug into the historical and biblical examples of courtship, I realized I was wrong. Modern Courtship is not in the Bible. Calling it "biblical dating" doesn't make it biblical.

Just because someone quotes the Bible in their book doesn't mean their system is biblical. And yes, that applies to this book. We must approach Scripture circumspectly.

When applying Scripture, particularly the Old Testament, to our lives, we have to differentiate between biblical practice, principle, and command. Just because Jacob had two wives and a seven-year engagement doesn't mean that God wants all men to have two wives and seven-year engagements.

What we have in the Old Testament are a lot of stories: each one different from the others.

Sometimes a woman is the protagonist in a romance (such as Ruth with Boaz) and at other times the man takes the lead (like Jacob with Rachel). There are arranged marriages (Isaac and Rebekah) and women who entered a marriage through a harem (David and Abigail, Michal, Bathsheba). Some women even chose their own husbands (Zelophehad's daughters).

> When applying Scripture, particularly the Old Testament, to our lives, we have to differentiate between biblical practice, principle, and command.

There are some good scriptural precepts about sexual purity in 1 Corinthians 6:12–20, and there are some principles about the benefits of marrying young in Psalm 127, but no examples of Modern Courtship.

In fact, many of the stories in the Bible violate basic tenets of courtship. For instance, the very first thing Jacob does when he sees Rachel is to run up and kiss her (Genesis 29:11). I don't think many courtship communities would approve of that kind of physical contact. They didn't save their first kiss for the altar. *Gasp!*

The Bible is surprisingly quiet when it comes to laying out a system of courtship. In fact, Jesus even qualified the Old Testament marriage laws when he said the divorce code was written because of the hardness of the Israelites' hearts (Matthew 19:8).

> Many of the stories in the Bible violate basic tenets of courtship.

The apostle Paul, who is usually very direct, speaks with all kinds of qualifiers when talking about romantic relationships. He makes a special point to say that not all of his instructions are from the Lord in 1 Corinthians 7:25–28. I can't think of another topic where Paul is this cautious with his words.

How can we say with certainty that a courtship system is biblical when even the biblical writers hesitate to do so? Could it be that God expects courtship systems to reflect the culture of the folks getting married?

Even more interesting, most of the moral arguments for Modern Courtship are actually arguments *for* Arranged Marriage. Arguments for strong involvement of parents fit Arranged Marriage much better than they fit Modern Courtship. Arranged Marriage also has a clearer biblical precedent and a more proven track record.

If you want to follow the examples of the Bible, Arranged Marriage is your safest bet. But let me be clear: nowhere in the Bible does it say "Thou shalt have an arranged marriage."

When I started PracticalCourtship.com, one of my goals was to never use the site to criticize Arranged Marriage. In countries like India, which have both Arranged Marriages and "Love Marriages," the Arranged Marriages have the lower divorce rate. Arranged Marriage has been used by many cultures for many years, so who am I to criticize those cultures?

But I am not convinced Arranged Marriage is a good fit for Western culture. Many Americans value individual liberty more than life itself. We're not comfortable giving this important decision to someone else. Because of that, parents hesitate to arrange marriages lest their children resent them if the marriage turns out to be unhappy.

> **Q&A #8**
> Are you saying that we can rely solely on human wisdom in relationships?

Suffice it to say that I don't see Arranged Marriage taking off in America except in a handful of subcultures.

We need a system to help young people make good decisions. While I believe that Modern Courtship's proponents intended for it to be that solution, I now realize it has caused more problems than we expected.

Modern Courtship intended to take us "back to our roots." It, in fact, did just the opposite.

Is Modern Courtship a Recipe for Lifelong Singleness?

Some people argue, "But courtship works! It worked for so-and-so, and they're happily married." You likely know a handful of couples who found marriage through Modern Courtship. But if the system *really* worked, you would know *dozens and dozens* of happily married couples, thanks to Modern Courtship.

The Baby Boomers created the rules of courtship out of fear. They wanted to protect their children from the mistakes they made during the Sexual Revolution and its aftermath. The rules came from good intentions.

During the 1990s and early 2000s, millions of young people embraced the tenets of courtship in part or in whole. And it's no wonder why—in a culture where we demonized dating, and divorce ran rampant, Modern Courtship seemed like the only alternative.

Many of those young people are still single today, but they don't have to be.

If you're one of the millions of frustrated singles, there's hope for you: there's an easier path to marriage that's more fun and still honors God.

If we want to get back to the marriage rates of our grandparents, we need to learn from them and adopt their approach. It's my hope that the Traditional Dating practiced by our grandparents will be part of the solution to resolving the Courtship Crisis.

5

PURITY, SEX, AND JESUS-FLAVORED BUBBLEGUM

When I was in high school, a local youth group hosted an evangelism event. They brought in a guest preacher and a special band. A friend handed me a stack of flyers, and I helped him pass them out.

I remember sitting in the back of a basketball gym, listening to the guest preacher rail against the evil and power of sin. He told us that if we lost our purity, we were like tape that had lost its stickiness or gum that had lost its flavor. He didn't give us a rose to grow tattered as we passed it from person to person. But he might as well have. Maybe he would have, if more people had been there. The flyers hadn't worked and the gym was mostly empty.

His anger and frustration still stick with me all these years later. Perhaps the empty chairs were getting to him.

He told us that God commands us to maintain our purity through strength of character, discipline, and avoidance of temptation. Young women bore the responsibility of keeping young men from thinking lustful thoughts, so they had to dress modestly at all times lest they defraud the men around them.

I left the gym feeling like a terrible person. I wanted to honor God, but I felt nothing I could do would please Him. I felt doomed that God would be forever disappointed in me.

From the expressions of those around me, they felt the same way. Few of us met this man's standards. I realized later that the speaker was one of many "purity preachers" common in those days—preachers who knew more about the mechanics of purity than how to inspire young people to live joyful, godly lives.

Purity Matters

You won't find any rants against purity in this book. Holiness is important to God. An entire Testament of the Bible focuses on the topic of righteousness. Walking in purity yields many benefits, and sin has consequences.

Deep down, we know this is true. The law is written on our consciences, after all (Romans 2:15). We know it's wrong to lie, steal, murder, or commit adultery. The psalmist tells us that we can keep our way pure by shaping it according to God's word (Psalms 119:9). The Bible is clear that the righteous are blessed and the wicked are cursed.

I, for one, prefer divine blessing, given the choice. But are guilt and shame the biblical path to purity?

> Many young Christians have been hurt by the evangelical purity movement.

Many young Christians have been hurt by the evangelical purity movement. Some young people tried so hard to guard their purity they shut themselves off from the outside world. The guilt and shame drummed up by purity preachers caused others to do away with purity altogether.

Many young people ask, "If purity is something I can lose, then once I lose it, why try anymore?"

One woman told me, "When I started dating my husband, we decided right away that purity wasn't important to us. We'd both been in really stressful courtships with strict purity rules and were completely done with that stress. So we chose to forge our own path and make our own decisions in regard to purity."

I've heard many stories like this, of singles who, after being burned by Modern Courtship, embraced Modern Dating.

Another woman said, "I broke up with a man who I would've otherwise married, because we had crossed lines in regard to the physical aspect of our relationship. My boyfriend didn't think what we were doing was wrong—we never had sex— but I felt so much guilt and shame. I felt like breaking up was the only way out of the sin I found myself entangled in."

> A strong focus on the rules can backfire.

I don't want to condone impure relationships. But I do want to show that a strong focus on the rules can backfire. Modern Courtship calls those who break its man-made rules "sinners." This leads to shame more than it leads to purity.

In Romans 8, we learn that there is no condemnation in Christ. And while that certainly doesn't give us license to throw out righteousness, it does show us that crippling guilt and shame aren't from God. Jesus wants something more for His followers when it comes to purity.

Throwing Stones for Purity

A particular group of people in the New Testament focused primarily on purity. They turned Old Testament passages into weapons. They weren't the heroes of the gospels. In fact, Jesus got into more fights with these Purity Police than with any other group. Consider this passage from John 8:3–11:

> As he was speaking, the teachers of religious law and the Pharisees brought a woman who had been caught in the act of adultery. They put her in front of the crowd.
>
> "Teacher," they said to Jesus, "this woman was caught in the act of adultery. The law of Moses says to stone her. What do you say?"
>
> They were trying to trap him into saying something they could use against him, but Jesus stooped down and wrote in the dust with his finger. They kept demanding an answer, so he stood up again and said, "All right, but let the one who has never sinned throw the first stone!" Then he stooped down again and wrote in the dust.
>
> When the accusers heard this, they slipped away one by one, beginning with the oldest, until only Jesus was left in the middle of the crowd with the woman. Then Jesus stood up again and said to the woman, "Where are your accusers? Didn't even one of them condemn you?"
>
> "No, Lord," she said.
>
> And Jesus said, "Neither do I. Go and sin no more."

Our desire to look pure tempts us to take an area in which we feel holy and turn it into a rock to throw at people who struggle in that area. For example, if a man doesn't struggle with lying, then looking down on liars may make him feel better. He just needs to ignore the fact that God hates haughty eyes (Proverbs 6:16–17).

Or conversely, someone who struggles with a sin may look down on those who struggle more and will create strong rules about that area. Instead of admitting their own weakness, they clothe themselves in self-righteousness, hoping it will protect them from the cold wind of temptation.

I know this because I used to be a passionate member of the Purity Police. I felt quite superior to everyone who dated. Even on my worst day, at least I didn't date. If I'd been alive during Jesus's day, I'm sure I would've been standing with stone in hand with the rest of them. It took years for God to open my eyes that this did not work. It didn't help me and it didn't help others.

As more people in a community turn into Purity Police, the pressure to wear a mask of holiness grows. So we put on our purity rings, wash away our makeup, and make sure every denim skirt falls below every knee. Kissing is forbidden until the wedding day and no hand-holding until engagement. The most pure have a "hands-off" courtship where even side-hugs are forbidden until marriage. Oh, and chaperones, lots and lots of chaperones.

I know young people who dreaded going to homeschool events because the pressure to "look righteous" was more than they could handle. At these events, their parents would punish them for every minor infraction in an attempt to coerce them into purity.

Purity Police don't punish just those within the community for bad conduct. They also chase away the unclean. "If you can't sign our statement of faith, you can't play sports with us," is their battle cry.

They're convinced that if an unclean child is allowed to interact with their clean child, the result will be that their child becomes unclean. This is Old Testament thinking.

In the Old Testament, if a clean man touched a leper, he became unclean. In the New Testament, when Jesus or one of His followers touched a leper, the leper was made clean.

Is it possible to focus so much on purity that we lose sight of the Gospel?

By chasing away the "lepers," we're creating a culture of guilt and shame that destroys the very relationships we wish to cherish. Jesus embraced the kind of people the Purity Police try to chase away.

> Is it possible to focus so much on purity that we lose sight of the Gospel?

I've noticed that once someone goes through a "failed courtship," they often get labeled as "damaged goods" because they've "given their hearts away." It's extremely rare to find someone who had a Modern Courtship called off and went on to successfully court someone else to marriage. So in addition to chasing away outsiders, we also chase away our own wounded.

We Are All Damaged Goods

This purity culture is particularly tragic because none of us are pure. The Bible tells us our righteousness is as pure before God as a used tampon is to us (Isaiah 64:6). Sorry for the gross analogy, but that's the modern equivalent of "filthy rags."

We are all tape that has lost its stickiness. We are all bubblegum that has lost its flavor. What right do any of us have to stand in judgment when we've all sinned? Who of us can cast the first stone?

Could that guest preacher have been wrong? Do strength of character, discipline, and avoiding temptation really make us pure? Do girls dressing modestly keep men pure? Does "not kissing till the wedding day" make a marriage pure?

My understanding of the teachings of Jesus is that our

action or inaction isn't going to make us pure. Righteousness doesn't come from the Purity Police enforcing the rules. We can't beat one another into purity. It only comes from the Spirit of Christ living in our hearts. If the Holy Spirit isn't in us, following the rules is like painting a coffin in an attempt to make the corpse stop stinking.

> We are all tape that has lost its stickiness. We are all bubblegum that has lost its flavor.

Or put another way, Jesus is the stickiness of my tape. Jesus is the flavor of my bubblegum. Jesus is my only hope on the Day of Judgment. There is no plan B.

Who Should Enforce the Rules?

What should we do if we see someone sinning? Do we need to punish them for that sin? Is it our responsibility to ensure that every sin has its consequence? That every sinner wears her scarlet letter? At what point do we need to call in the Purity Police?

In my life, positive change hasn't come through someone enforcing the rules. It happened when the Holy Spirit corrected me, in His way and in His timing. Sure, someone can try to force me to act right, but that kind of intrusion seldom lasts. But if God convicts me in His gentle, loving way, the change sticks.

The most surprising thing to me about Jesus is how gentle and patient He is in correcting me. He's more gentle with me than I am with others. He's especially more gentle than I am with myself.

There are sins I've struggled with for years, yet He has never once given up on me, never once stopped helping me to be better. He's always there when I stumble, and He puts me back on my feet to try again.

Sometimes a fault of mine seems so obvious to others, yet it's not what Jesus is working on in my heart at that time. Thank God that He doesn't try to fix every imperfection all at once. I don't think I could survive that. I don't know if anyone could.

> The most surprising thing to me about Jesus is how gentle and patient He is in correcting me.

Who are we to dictate to God what sins He should address in others and in what order? Should we take matters into our own hands and handle the job of convicting others of sin?

The difference between conviction and condemnation isn't in what is said but in where it comes from. If it comes from the Holy Spirit, it's conviction. If it comes from a human (or from ourselves), it's condemnation.

Can God speak through humans? Absolutely. But there's a big difference between God speaking through man and man speaking for God. If God is speaking through man, He'll confirm His words in our hearts.

As I listened to Galatians, I realized that, for me, courtship was like circumcision for the Galatians. It looked like a shortcut to holiness when in reality it was a detour of pride. I relied on Modern Courtship to make me holy rather than relying on the Holy Spirit. What's worse is that I tried to force it on others. I finally had to drop my stone and walk away. Once I did, an amazing lightness overtook my heart.

I now have to trust God to take the specks from the eyes of those around me. He doesn't need my help for that. I also need to trust that He'll help me with the log in my own eye (Matthew 7:3–5).

What would the Church look like if we prayed for those struggling instead of policing them? What if we waited for God to convict them directly rather than trying to force them to comply with our rules? What if I were as patient with others as God has been patient with me?

My friend Mary DeMuth tells a story of her friend Randy who led a friend of his to Christ. We'll call him Bob. Friends pestered Randy to tell Bob it was wrong to sleep with his girlfriend.

> What would the Church look like if we prayed for those struggling instead of policing them?

Randy held firm. "No, if I convict him, he'll always need to come to me to figure out his life. But if God convicts him, he'll learn to trust God for everything."

A few weeks later, Bob showed up on Randy's doorstep, sleeping bag in hand. "I just read that it's wrong to have sex before marriage, and God convicted me. Can I stay on your couch?"

A Time to Speak Out and a Time to Keep Quiet

I'm not saying we should never speak up about sin. If someone is sinning against us, Jesus gives us a clear protocol of when and how to say something in Matthew 18.

If someone sins against us, the first thing we should do is to talk to them directly. In my experience, most of the time this is all you need to do to take care of the problem. Usually the person who has done wrong will apologize, repent, make restitution if needed, and take steps to ensure that it won't happen again.

If not, you approach them again with one or two others. If they still refuse to repent, you bring them before the whole church.

There's also a time to speak up for those who can't speak for themselves (Proverbs 31:8). We have a responsibility to protect the weakest among us from wolves, especially when those predators are wearing the clothes of the Purity Police.

If someone has broken human law, they may need to go before human authorities so justice can be served. Just because God has forgiven you for stealing doesn't mean you shouldn't make restitution to the one you robbed.

Protect yourself and others from harm. Otherwise, trust God to be God. He'll convict people of sin in His timing. The Holy Spirit has this job covered. God doesn't need us to serve as His police force.

> **Q&A #9**
> Is it okay to kiss?

One woman told me, "I don't like 'purity' language because it implies that one mistake can soil a person and make them less worthy of love and relationship than someone who hasn't made the same mistake. I also personally believe that sexual mistakes don't make a person any more 'impure' than other sins such as pride and selfishness. Shouldn't we hold one another to a standard of righteousness that encompasses every area of our lives?"

It's hard to argue that we shouldn't strive for righteousness in every area of our lives. Isolating one kind of sin as a "super sin" and then feeling holy because we avoid that sin is a detour around true holiness. Sanctification is a process, and when we skip that process, we shortchange our spiritual growth.

Is Sex Evil?

Nope.

Sex is a lot of things, but evil isn't one of them. On a very basic level, sex has the chance of bringing an immortal being into the universe. That's amazing when you think about it. In light of eternity, having sex may be one of the most significant things most people ever do.

God's first words to humans in the Bible are a command-ment to have sex—enough sex to fill the planet with people (Genesis 1:28).

What's more, the Bible talks quite frankly about sex, not only as a means for reproduction but also as a covenant act between a married couple, created to bring intimacy, oneness, and yes, even fun. In fact, an entire book of the Bible is a celebration of sex: Song of Songs.

Yet purity culture tells us that both sex and sexual at-traction are evil. The entire focus is wrong. If having sex within mar-riage is a biblically ordained and God-honoring act, then can longing for it be wrong? How can longing to obey God be evil?

> We have a respon-sibility to pro-tect the weakest among us from wolves, especially when those pred-ators are wearing the clothes of the Purity Police.

The Purity Police think that if they can make sex look dirty and dangerous, young people will be less likely to fool around. In reality, sex within marriage is a beautiful banquet, a taste of heaven to come. If we focus on the banquet, we won't be tempted by the dumpster of premarital or extramarital sex.

When we focus on the rules, our attention is focused on the dumpster rather than the banquet. In many churches, it's taboo for married couples to talk about sex but okay for the preacher to preach against fornication. The focus is off. If all we think about is the dumpster, we can begin to believe that eating trash is our only option.

The lie that sex is evil fills young people with guilt, shame, and fear. It destroys something that God created to be beautiful. It can also create challenges for couples once they get married.

One woman, Lindsay, said, "The morning after my wedding, I found myself sobbing in the shower, scrubbing myself raw because I felt so unclean, so dirty. I had allowed myself to become so entrenched in staying pure that when I finally lost that purity—in the exact way God had intended—I felt as if I had committed my greatest sin.

"It took me years of counseling to be able to enjoy sex with my husband," she said. "Not because I didn't love him or because I wasn't attracted to him, but because I carried so closely to my heart the shame and guilt I associated with sex."

> God's first words to humans in the Bible are a commandment to have sex—enough sex to fill the planet with people.

Once someone is convinced that sex is evil, how can he or she enjoy having it? An hour-long marriage ceremony cannot undo a lifetime of trying not to think about the dumpster. This can create marital trouble as the marriage's foundation is being formed. This focus on the dumpster hurts both singles who harbor hopes for healthy relationships and married couples who should be enjoying fulfilling, intimate sex.

According to the Bible, God wants us to get married and then have a lot of sex—enough sex to multiply and fill the earth. Enough sex to build strong, intimate marriages that stand the test of time. Enough sex to cause married couples to hold hands under the table, to wink at each other across the room, and to race home to each other's embrace.

We'd do ourselves a lot of favors as a community if we put more effort into making marital sex sound amazing. If we focus more on saying yes to marital sex, it will be easier to say no to premarital and extramarital sex.

If we focus on God's clear instructions about sex and marriage, we'll easily see the joy, the intimacy, and the love that God wants each of us to experience. We'll also be able to let go of the guilt and shame that has so deeply ensnared us.

Play It as You See It

One of the things I learned about playing chess is that you have to play the board as you see it and not how you wish it was. If you make a mistake and lose a rook, don't send in your knight, trying to justify one bad move with another bad move.

In the game of life, we all make mistakes. We know the rules, and we know deep down when we've broken them. We have moves we'd take back if we could. But no DeLorean is going to roll up and give us a do-over. We can't change the past.

That doesn't mean some of us don't try. I can torture myself with regrets and self-hatred, but that won't change the past. I've been there. It didn't help. When I'm honest with myself, I can see there's no way to win with the board as it is.

It's only a matter of time before sin declares "checkmate." It could be in two moves. It could be in ten. We've already lost, even if we can't see it yet. The only way to win is not to play.

> If we focus more on saying yes to marital sex, it will be easier to say no to premarital and extramarital sex.

Here's some good news. We don't have to play anymore. There's a heavenly Chessmaster who can take over. When we're baptized into Christ, our old self and all those past mistakes die with Him. The old is gone. It's locked away in the tomb and forgotten.

Then the new is come. When we give Jesus our pieces, we're born again as new people. He sets us up with a new chess game and puts his Holy Spirit in our hearts to guide us as we play.

It's not too late to surrender your pieces to Jesus. But understand that making him Lord of your life means He gets to move all the pieces, not just the ones that are in trouble. But who better to run your game than the Game's Creator?

All you have to do is ask Him to take over. He can give you your fresh start today.

PART 2

THE CASE FOR TRADITIONAL DATING

6

THE RULES OF TRADITIONAL DATING

My grandmother grew up in a marginally Christian community. People went to church on Sunday, but that was the extent of their religious activity. They weren't the daily Bible-reading, small-grouping, mission-tripping Christian young people common today in the courtship community.

And yet her friends all got married and stayed married for decades. What on earth did they do that worked so well? Curious to discover her secrets, I invited my grandmother to dinner and asked her to tell me more about her dating history.

She explained that when she went on dates in junior high (middle school), her parents had two main rules for her: Don't go out with the same guy twice in a row, and be home by 10:00 PM. If she went out for soda with Bob on Tuesday, she had to go to a movie with Bill on Thursday before she could go to the school dance with Bob on Saturday.

That sounded crazy to me. Wasn't that cheating? Once you go on a date with someone, you can't go out with someone else until you first "break up." Can you?

I asked her about it. She explained that the lack of exclusivity helped them guard their hearts and kept them from getting too serious too quickly. The lack of pressure made relationships friendly and fun—not awkward and forced. How could a boy have a claim to her time, heart, or body if she was going out with someone else later that week?

> **Q&A #10**
> Are you saying that if I use Traditional Dating, I'll have a long and happy marriage like your grandparents?

"The guys wouldn't even want to kiss you!" she said. That surprised me, because one of the big arguments against dating is that it's so highly sexualized.

By the time my grandmother was in high school, she'd gone on dates with a dozen different guys. By the time she turned seventeen, she knew which Bob she wanted to "go steady" with. She married my grandfather when she was eighteen and he was twenty, and they stayed married until my grandfather passed away, fifty-three years later.

"If I had only gone out with one or two guys, I wouldn't have known what I wanted in a husband," she said.

This was such a foreign concept to my courtship-focused mind. How could good Christian parents encourage their children to go out on *multiple* dates with *multiple* people? And how could a system with so many dates not lead to compromise?

And perhaps most pressing, how come it *worked* when so many singles now struggle with courtship, which seems so holy and just?

Traditional Dating is based on two simple rules:

1. Don't Go Steady Too Soon
2. Don't Stay Out Too Late

Is that it? Just two rules?

As I talked with her, I realized the beautiful simplicity of this system. The more complicated a system is, the harder it is to follow. Traditional Dating made finding a good match easy, ethical, and fun.

I should point out that these are not biblical rules. You're not sinning if you break them. Following them won't make you holy. These are *common sense* rules handed down from our grandparents. It turns out that there's modern science behind their traditional common sense, as we will see later in this chapter.

> I should point out that these are not biblical rules. You're not sinning if you break them. Following them won't make you holy.

These rules are like a recipe. You can tweak them as needed. They're here to point you to a healthy relationship, but the rules themselves won't make your relationship healthy. These rules are like a handrail on a staircase. They exist to point you in the right direction and help keep you from falling. It's completely possible to climb the stairs without using the handrail.

As with all things, our common sense should yield to the guidance of the Holy Spirit. After all, sometimes God calls us to do uncommon-sense things. That said, these rules do not conflict with Christian doctrine. Millions of Christians used Traditional Dating to find their husband or wife. In fact, it could be argued that most of the heroes of the faith in the twentieth century followed Traditional Dating.

If the word "rules" freaks you out, you can think of these as practical guidelines.

Rule #1: Don't Go Steady Too Soon

James met Meredith at a Christmas party. They exchanged

numbers and started texting every day. They both loved Jesus and shared a passion for obscure Japanese anime.

After a wonderful six-hour date, they felt that they had even more to talk about than when they started. At the end of the date, James asked Meredith if she'd be his girlfriend. So far she liked everything about him and enjoyed spending time with him talking about mutual interests.

What should Meredith do?

Modern Dating says that if Meredith likes him, she should say yes. Modern Courtship says that once James gets permission from Meredith's father, then they can become a couple.

Traditional Dating, on the other hand, says that it's too soon to tell. Meredith needs to make a concerted effort to go out with other guys in addition to James.

> Getting too serious too soon is a problem that Modern Dating and Modern Courtship share.

Going on dates with these other guys will help Meredith know if James really is the kind of man she wants a relationship with. These other dates give her perspective while helping her guard her heart.

Getting too serious too soon is a problem that Modern Dating and Modern Courtship share.

Both of these systems result in singles going through one committed, heartbreaking relationship after another. They differ only in frequency and style of intensity.

Modern Dating is more physically intense, while Modern Courtship is often more emotionally intense. Going steady too soon is one of the leading causes of unnecessary heartbreak for young people.

This rule is hard to follow. The more you have feelings for someone, the more you want to spend time together and have them all to yourself. But as you enter that exclusive, committed relationship, you can grow blind to their faults.

There may come a day when love is blind, but it is not this day. You need your eyes wide open at first. Once you start going steady, it's easy to fall into the trap of thinking it's your only option. Also, the potential pain of leaving the relationship can keep you involved longer than necessary, and that leads to even more commitment and even more pain if you break up.

I recently talked with a young woman about her courtship. A guy in her church asked her father permission to court her. After getting a yes, he came to her at church and said, "I talked with your dad and we're courting now." Now that's what you call "a courtship romance." He didn't even bother to ask if *she* was okay with it!

She told me, "I felt like he was my only option. He was the only man to make it past my dad in five years. I felt that if I told him no, I'd never have another opportunity." So she "went steady" with him, as my grandmother would call it.

She didn't love him, but she felt her choices were between him or a lifetime of singleness. He had never won her heart, but the relationship hurled them toward greater commitment and greater heartbreak, nonetheless.

When a woman says no to going steady, she forces the man to keep fighting for her heart. Imagine that Meredith says, "James, I really enjoy spending time with you and I love talking about anime. I'd love to keep getting to know you, but I'm not ready to go steady yet."

How do you think James would respond? Most men are competitive. Knowing that Meredith is interested in him but not ready to go steady will inspire James to try even harder to win her heart.

It's important to mention how critical it is that Meredith conveys her feelings honestly. If she's not interested in

James, this is *not* the way to tell him. Girls who say no like this often find that the guy develops *more* interest in them.

Q&A #11
How do I say no to a second date without sounding mean or sending the wrong message?

By this point, James knows he has a solid chance with Meredith. He also knows that she may still go out with other guys. This combined knowledge will crystallize James's feelings and help him determine if she's worth fighting for. If he's not that into her, they can both prevent a painful breakup down the road by not going steady too soon.

Remember, once you become "a couple," the temptation to test boundaries also increases, so waiting to go steady also prevents unnecessary temptation. Exclusivity brings with it expectations and a greater risk for heartbreak. You need to let the relationship mature before you are ready to take that risk.

How Soon Is Too Soon to Go Steady?

Knowing when you're ready to go steady depends on how long you've been Traditionally Dating. The more people you go out with, the clearer idea you'll have of what you're looking for. The older you are and the more dates you've gone on, the sooner it becomes safe to go steady.

Let's say you go out with an intellectual person. Do you find the person mentally stimulating, or dry and boring? The best way to find this out is to go on a date with an intellectual person and see what you think.

What if you went out with a major sports fan? Would you share that person's interests, or would that turn you off? The only way to really know is to go to a game and find out.

What about being in a relationship with an outdoor enthusiast? Do you find long bike rides and hikes fun or boring? Why not go on a bike ride and find out?

If you go on a date and have a miserable time, the date was still valuable because now you have a better idea of what you *don't* want.

At the risk of sounding like a nerd, try to think of your dates as scientific research. Even failures lead to discoveries about yourself and others. I know this isn't the most romantic analogy, but if you think like a scientist, you might discover some chemistry.

> If you go on a date and have a miserable time, the date was still valuable because now you have a better idea of what you *don't* want.

Each date gives you clues about yourself and others. For some people, a date that consists of nothing but talking about politics is heaven. For others, it's a taste of a special hell reserved for people who talk at the theater. Each date gives you a "data point" that helps you paint a picture of the kind of person you fit best.

Rule #2: Don't Stay Out Too Late

Frank asks Alice to go to a Casting Crowns concert. She agrees, and on Friday night they attend the concert. They have a great time enjoying some awesome music and even singing along.

The concert ends around 10:30, and Frank mentions that he recently found a new frozen yogurt place that's open late. He asks if Alice wants to swing by and get some "froyo" before heading home.

What should she say?

She likes and trusts Frank. She likes frozen yogurt, and

tomorrow is a Saturday, so she can sleep in. What's wrong with doing one more thing tonight?

There are two reasons why Alice should say no to late-night froyo.

But first we need to talk about radishes.

Radishes, it turns out, can teach us something about willpower. Scientists like Roy Baumeister of Florida State University have been studying willpower for years. In one of Baumeister's studies, he asked people to participate in an experiment about taste perception.

The researchers set up a room filled with the aroma of freshly baked cookies. Study participants sat at a table with two plates: one had fresh cookies, and the other had raw radishes. The researchers split the participants into two groups. They asked one group to eat only the cookies and told the other to eat only the radishes. Then the researchers left the room.

But this study wasn't a study of taste perception at all. It was secretly a study of willpower.

The cookies tempted the radish-eaters to the extreme. Sometimes the radish-eaters even picked up a cookie and smelled it before returning it to the plate. But no one on "Team Radish" gave in to temptation and tasted a cookie. Their willpower held.

Most people can exercise their willpower for short periods of time, and this study showed that. But the study wasn't over.

The researchers then asked the participants to go into a second room to work on an unsolvable geometry puzzle. Which group worked harder on the test? Team Radish or Team Cookie?

Team Cookie averaged nineteen minutes of work on the

puzzle. Team Radish gave up after only eight minutes. Team Radish used up their willpower resisting the cookies, but Team Cookie had a full tank of willpower left, and they worked more than twice as long.

Baumeister shared the results of this and dozens of similar studies in his book *Willpower: Rediscovering the Greatest Human Strength.*[1] Willpower depletion is such a common phenomenon that scientists now have a term for it: ego depletion.

> The later it gets, the easier it is to make regrettable choices.

I don't think my grandparents knew anything about ego depletion. But they did have the common sense to know that the later it gets, the easier it is to make regrettable choices.

Know When to HALT

Another discovery Baumeister's scientists made is that we have just one "tank" of willpower to draw from. We don't have a "resisting junk food" tank and a separate "resisting a nap" tank. We draw from our sole willpower tank when we make decisions or resist impulses to eat, sleep, etc. It's important to realize when your willpower is running low and take precautions.

Alcoholics Anonymous teaches recovering alcoholics to avoid HALT situations when they are **H**ungry, **A**ngry, **L**onely, and **T**ired. These HALT states require alcoholics to make additional draws on their willpower reserves—willpower they need to resist alcohol.

For example, angry people must use extra willpower not to lash out at those around them. An angry alcoholic who exhausts his willpower reservoir by resisting the urge to cuss out his boss is more vulnerable to grabbing a drink on the way home from work.

Baumeister recommends that you use your willpower to

avoid situations where you'll need to use your willpower.

In *The Odyssey*, Odysseus and the sailors take precautions to avoid the temptation of the sirens' song. The sailors stuffed their ears with wax so the sirens wouldn't lure them near the coast where they'd dash their ship upon the rocks. Odysseus has the men tie him to the mast so he can listen without diving into the water.

Scientists call this a "pre-commitment strategy." Making a commitment ahead of time helps us avoid temptation without using as much willpower. This is what you do when you put your alarm clock on the other side of the bedroom. Your awake self is pre-committing your future, still-asleep self to wake up and not press snooze. When my grandparents agreed to be home by 10:00 PM, they practiced a pre-commitment strategy just like Odysseus and his men.

> As my grandfather used to say, "Nothing good ever happens after midnight."

Each morning after breakfast we have a relatively full tank of willpower. We tend to be our best selves in the morning. We're more likely to exercise and eat healthy foods, and we're less likely to sit in front of the TV eating potato chips.

As the day progresses, we have to use our willpower to make decisions. We resist taking a nap, or we resist buying candy from the vending machine. The later in the day it gets, the less willpower remains in the tank.

If Alice says yes to late-night froyo, she's putting herself in a situation where both she and Frank will likely have depleted willpower tanks. The sooner they call it a night, the less likely they are to make decisions they'll regret in the morning.

As my grandfather used to say, "Nothing good ever happens after midnight."

My grandmother told me her father often sat on the steps of her house waiting for her to get home. He knew that if she got home before her willpower tank ran empty, there was little chance for morning regrets.

As my father often told me, "He who hoots with the owls at night cannot soar with the eagles by day."

How to Exercise Your Willpower

Professor Baumeister makes the case that willpower is like a muscle. In the short-term, using willpower reduces the willpower remaining for other tasks just like lifting a heavy weight makes your muscles tired.

> "He who hoots with the owls at night cannot soar with the eagles by day."

But over time, using your willpower builds your overall willpower capacity. After a hard workout, lifting your arms to wash your hair can be a challenge. But after a month of working out, you can lift weights you could never lift before.

Going on dates and coming home early gives singles a chance to build their willpower reserves. Traditional Dating is like going to the gym and working out your willpower muscles.

Don't Eat the Seed Corn

The second reason Alice should say no to froyo has nothing to do with radishes, but it does have to do with farming.

There's an old saying among farmers to "never eat your seed corn." If you eat all your corn, you won't have anything to sow next planting season. Smart farmers set aside seed corn for the next year's planting. This same principle applies to relationships.

If Alice likes Frank, she'll save some seed corn for the next date. If every date ends with more topics to discuss, then the next date will soon follow. She can keep the relationship from getting stale by always saving something interesting to talk about for the next date. If Frank is interested in Alice, he'll save fun activities for the next date as well.

> A savvy woman leaves the man wanting more at the end of every date.

A savvy woman leaves the man wanting more at the end of every date. A smart man does the same.

In this case, fleeing temptation is the kind of savvy move recommended in popular dating books like *The Rules* and *Not Your Mother's Rules* by Ellen Fein and Sherrie Schneider. These books recommend that women limit first dates to no more than two hours and limit texting too. Their reasoning has nothing to do with temptation and everything to do with making women more attractive by making them scarce.

The idea in those books is that if a man wants to talk to you, he needs to ask you out on a date and not just text all day long. If he wants to talk with you longer, he needs to ask you on another date. This can move women out of the "friendzone" and into the "wifezone."

How Late Is Too Late for a Date?

My grandmother has started dating again (my grandfather passed away over a decade ago). When I hear she has a date, I make sure to tell her, "Don't stay out too late." The quizzical look she gives me is priceless. There's something funny about telling someone in her eighties not to stay out too late. It's one of those jokes that's funny to me every time.

This rule is vague on purpose. "Too late" varies by age and maturity. "Too late" will be different for an eighteen-year-old than for an eighty-year-old. Remember, willpower is like a muscle. The more time you've spent building that muscle, the later you can stay out without trouble.

As a general rule of thumb, I recommend "earlier than you would like." My grandparents had to be home by 10:00 PM. Even Cinderella had to be home by midnight. Notice in that story how the prince searched for her after she left early. She left him wanting more. Take a lesson from Cinderella if you want Prince Charming to chase after you.

A friend of mine never had a curfew. Her parents wanted her to decide what the best time was for her to get home. So every time she left the house, they'd ask "Where are you going and when will you be home?" She'd tell them, and then they'd ask, "And do you think that's an appropriate time based on the circumstances?"

This taught her to consider her actions and temptations. This also taught her to create her own pre-commitment strategy. As an adult, she learned to make stronger choices. I know women who will schedule another activity two hours after a date. This is their way of pre-committing to keeping the date to no longer than two hours.

Before you leave the house, consider asking yourself the same questions: When will I be home? Is that an appropriate time considering the circumstances?

First Things First

One day in college I found myself running late for class, so I threw on a shirt and buttoned it as I rushed out the door. After enough strange looks from people on the quad, I looked at my reflection in a nearby window.

My shirt was totally crooked. One collar angled up nearly to my ear. I'd left in such a hurry that the buttons were all out of place. If I had paid attention to the first button, the rest would've fallen into place without much thought.

#CourtshipInCrisis

There's no law that you have to button the top button of a shirt first. Many people start in the middle and the buttons line up just fine. But starting with the first button is a *common sense* rule that makes buttoning a shirt easy. Most of us learned this rule from our mothers when we were young, or we figured it out through trial and error. It's when I thought I didn't need to follow common sense rules that I ended up walking through campus with a crooked shirt.

You already know what is and isn't appropriate on a date. The problem isn't knowledge. If you read the Bible and allow the Holy Spirit to guide you, your conscience will tell you right from wrong. Knowing the right thing to do and doing the right thing are as different as a toddler knowing how to wipe his bottom and actually wiping it.

> You already know what is and isn't appropriate on a date.

Traditional Dating's rules "Don't Go Steady Too Soon" and "Don't Stay Out Too Late" are designed to help you do what you already know you should do. They'll help you avoid the kind of weak moments that lead to a lifetime of regrets and make it easier to find the love of your life. Together with the steps from Chapter 7, they'll help you build a happy marriage that can last a lifetime.

As Meredith says no to going steady too soon and Alice stays no to froyo too late, they are both saying yes to healthy relationships.

7

TRADITIONAL DATING: STEP BY STEP

One of the initiation rites in my Boy Scout troop was to start a campfire. On my first campout, the patrol leader tapped me to go first. Perhaps someone had told him about the "gasoline incident" on my grandparents' ranch.

"Where's the lighter fluid?" I asked.

"We don't use that Girl Scout water here," the patrol leader said. "This is the Boy Scouts, and we build our campfires from scratch. But since this is your first time, you can use more than one match." The scouts in my troop didn't hold a high opinion of the Girl Scouts, despite the vocal complaints of some of the troop moms.

One match? How on earth did they start a fire with just one match? After going through half the box of matches, I realized that it didn't matter how many matches I used if I didn't know how to start a fire. I fantasized about using a flamethrower, but that apparently violated the Boy Scout principle of "safety first."

The Boy Scout secret to starting a fire with only one match is lint. Pocket lint, belly-button lint, dryer lint—any kind of lint. We learned to collect dryer lint in Ziploc Baggies at home to bring on campouts. The Boy Scout motto, "Be Prepared," could be summarized by saying, "Know first aid, have a Swiss Army knife, and keep a pocket full of lint."

Dry lint can catch on fire from just one match. It burns hot and steady long enough to catch twigs on fire. Once the twigs start burning, you add larger twigs. Work your way up to sticks, and then add dry logs.

Building a fire is all about heat management. Too little heat and the fire dies. Too much heat and you burn down the forest.

Fire is the foundation of civilization. Without it, we couldn't eat meat or charge our cell phones (most electricity comes from fire). Fires can be life-giving or deadly. In this way, they're a lot like relationships.

> Like a fire, what starts a relationship is not what sustains it.

Relationships can be life-giving or soul-crushing. They're the foundation of civilization and a cause of civilization-ending wars. Like a fire, what starts a relationship is not what sustains it. A man may fall in love with a woman's smile, but after sixty years, when her teeth are missing, he loves something deeper about her.

Relationships burn hot and fast at first. Over time, though, the fire needs slow-burning logs to burn reliably.

Putting a huge log on a young campfire can kill it. What can blow a mature fire into a hot flame can blow out a match. You need to give the match time to light the lint and the lint time to light the twigs and so on.

The steps of Traditional Dating are comparable to the steps of starting a fire.

The steps are:

1. Dating (Lint)
2. Going Steady (Twigs)
3. Engagement (Branches)
4. Marriage (Logs)

Each step burns best when soaked in prayer.

Step 1: Dating

Matt and Sarah met at a church softball game. They laughed their way through the third inning while the "Holy Hitters" demonstrated their complete lack of running ability with a failed slide at second base. Afterward, Matt asked Sarah if they could go out and grab some lemonade. She said yes, and they chatted about the game and life in general.

A few weeks later, Matt asked Sarah out again, but this time, they went bowling. By the time they reached the third frame, both realized they weren't bowling strikes. Matt's competitive nature annoyed Sarah, and long lulls in their conversations proved that they had little in common besides a love of softball and Jesus.

> The first step of Traditional Dating is just that—dating. Its purpose is to help a couple find out if they like each other.

Though they had fun bowling, they didn't go out again. They still see each other from time to time at church. They managed to find out, in a relatively painless way, that they weren't the best fit. They did it without the drama, awkwardness, and pain usually associated with Modern Dating. After all, they went on only two dates.

The first step of Traditional Dating is just that—dating.

Its purpose is to help a couple find out if they like each other.

Compare this to Modern Courtship where Matt would have had to work up the courage to go through Sarah's father. He would need to be ready to enter a relationship, for the purpose of marriage. All this in order to find out whether he and Sarah would be a good match. Modern Courtship would've changed a fun and painless night into a drawn-out relationship that ended in heartbreaking disappointment.

This step is like the lint I used to start fires in Boy Scouts. Lint lights quickly, but if you don't add more fuel, it burns out just as fast. If a couple in Step 1 doesn't find something more substantial, the fire simply burns out. And that's okay.

Like Matt and Sarah's relationship, if you let a lint fire burn out, not much is lost. Emotions aren't raw, friendships aren't destroyed, promises aren't broken. Matt and Sarah simply stopped, said goodbye, and moved on.

> It's hard to get to know someone's heart while running around an Ultimate Frisbee field.

The goal of Step 1 is to get to know yourself as much as it is to get to know the kind of person you'd fit well with. Sarah now knows that she may not be a great fit with a super-competitive guy. This helps her know what to look for in her next date.

Step 1 is as simple as that: Lots of singles go on lots of dates. The more people you go out with, the better you learn to know yourself and the kind of person you fit with. At the same time, you can get feedback and coaching from your friends and family.

Feedback from your family is important to Step 1. My grandmother said her father made a special point to meet each man before the date. Likewise, Sarah talked with her mom about her date with Matt.

Her mom wanted to know, "What did you like about him? What didn't you like?" Instead of trying to control the relationship, Sarah's mom saw her role as a coach to help her daughter learn to make good decisions, since she knew she wouldn't always be around to tell her daughter what to do.

In Traditional Dating, Step 1 is platonic. It's about getting to know someone as a person. The focus centers on personalities and common interests, not on the physical aspect of the relationship.

The goal of Step 1 is to help young people answer the following questions:

- Who am I?
- Who are you?
- Do I like you?
- Do you like me?
- What do our families think?

For high schoolers in my grandmother's era, the date traditionally started with the young man coming by the young woman's house. He knocked on the door, popped in, and met her parents. After a short conversation, the couple headed off together to dinner or some sort of fun activity like Putt-Putt golf, roller skating, or bowling. He then brought her home by a pre-arranged time set by her parents.

Q&A #12
Are double dates a good idea?

In college and beyond, parents were typically less involved than when their children were minors, but they still served as sounding boards for their kids regarding the above questions.

The modern trend has moved away from Step 1 dating and toward "group dating." This trend extends outside the

Church. Group dating is one of the few activities that Modern Courtship and Modern Dating Share.

That's unfortunate because, in general, group settings make it harder to answer questions like "Do I like you?" It's hard to get to know someone's heart while running around an Ultimate Frisbee field.

My grandmother went on lots of group activities in her day. But those group activities were fundamentally different because of one fact: everyone came to the group event as a couple. Today, people go to a dance as a group, whereas in my grandmother's day they would've gone to the dance as couples.

Step 2: Going Steady

Claire and Jesse had known each other for years. They grew up on the same street and spent their childhoods roaming the forest behind their houses, building a fortress out of branches and twigs.

Claire reigned queen of the fortress, making sure the dirt floor stayed clear of leaves and that the plastic water jug stayed full and ready for mud pie-making. Meanwhile, Jesse spent his days building up the walls and keeping watch from a secret perch on the bottom branch of the biggest pine tree they could find.

When Claire and Jesse got to high school, they naturally gravitated toward each other. Jesse asked her to the homeschool formal their freshman year, and a few weeks later on Friday night, he took her out to dinner after golf practice. They clearly liked each other. But was there more?

At first, Claire rejected the idea of Jesse as her "steady beau" and went on dates with several other guys. She went to a local college basketball game with Ben and out for frozen yogurt with Randy. But she always found herself gravitating toward Jesse. And he kept finding her. There was just something between the two of them that worked.

Jesse took Claire out to dinner and asked if she would be

his girlfriend. She said yes, and from then on, they went together to homeschool basketball games and church events.

A couple going steady is like the baby fire of twigs that the lint set aflame. The fire is very vulnerable in this step, and you have to watch closely to see what the fire needs to grow.

This is perhaps the most exciting and the most exhausting step as small flames of love slowly rise, hopefully into a full-blown fire. The last thing you want to do at this point is to pour the gasoline of a sexual relationship onto the baby flame.

This second step typically starts with an "ask" of some sort by the young man. In this "ask," the young man asks if the young woman would like to be his girlfriend. In my grandmother's day, high-school-aged singles would ask permission from their parents before going steady. Adult singles did not ask permission.

Step 2 is exclusive. "Going steady" means you aren't going out with anyone else. During a breakup, couples used to say, "I think we should start seeing other people." Or in other words, "We should stop going steady."

> If you're not ready to identify publicly as a couple, you're not ready to go steady.

In this step, you publicly identify yourselves as a couple. In the 1950s, the sign of exclusivity was when the guy gave the girl his letter jacket or fraternity pin. My grandmother can still remember where she was standing when my grandfather gave her his pin. When she wore the pin, it told the world that she was "his girl." It was a public symbol that she wasn't available for dates with other guys.

The modern equivalent to this would be to change your Facebook relationship status to "in a relationship." This allows the community around you to see you as a couple. It signals to other suitors that you're "off the market" as my grandmother would say. If you're not ready to identify publicly as a couple, you're not ready to go steady.

If Step 1 is about answering the question "Am I interested in you?" then Step 2 is about answering the question "Are we a good match?"

The goal of this Step 2 is to answer the following questions:

- Do we work as a couple?
- Does our community like us as a couple?

Family and community feedback is key to going steady. While love may be blind, your family and friends can still see clearly. If you want to hide your relationship status from your community, that's a sign something may be wrong or that you aren't ready to go steady.

One of the common "modifications" within Modern Courtship is for couples to keep their relationship a secret from friends until the engagement. Couples do this because they fear their community will blow out the fire of their budding relationship with expectations, pressure, and meddling.

It's critical that communities tend these young flames in a healthy way so couples don't feel the need to hide. Otherwise couples will be tempted to keep their relationships secret, which is bad for everyone.

There are three problems with keeping your relationship secret:

1. You spend less time with other friends.
2. You miss out on community feedback.

3. You miss out on mediators.

For more about secret relationships see Q&A #7.

Step 3: Engagement

Going back to our fire analogy, engagements represent branches you add to the fire once the twigs are burning well. These branches will ignite the solid logs of marriage.

Engagements are exciting and romantic. They symbolize that a couple has finally arrived at the place they've yearned to reach for so long. The couple is ready to make a lifelong commitment to each other.

Think about some of the proposals you've seen on YouTube. Proposal videos go viral not only because they're mushy and romantic, but also because they symbolize something so essential to each of us: strong, healthy relationships.

Engagement has survived more-or-less intact through the turbulence of the Sexual Revolution and the conservative counter-revolution. Engagement in Modern Courtship isn't much different from engagement in Traditional Dating.

Step 3 is about planning the wedding and creating a life together. As my accountant father says, "The devil is in the details." In this step, couples go through the details of life like learning how to handle conflict and how to communicate. It's the little foxes that ruin the vineyard of love (Song of Songs 2:15), and this step requires couples to hunt down those little foxes before they get a chance to do mischief to the impending marriage.

My parents still talk about how helpful their premarital counseling with Pastor Jack was in keeping them together for over thirty-five years. As my mom says, a lot of problems can be "nipped in the bud" in good premarital counseling so they are not allowed to grow into marriage-threatening issues.

Step 4: Marriage—A Beautiful Destination

There's an old Russian saying that says, "There are three pleasurable things to watch: the flowing of a river, the burning of a fire, and someone else working." Fires can be fun to watch and fun to build. Relationships are the same way.

Just remember that fires take work and must grow to a certain point in order to survive. Dating is a fun starting point, a place where relationships ignite, but that's not where you want to stay. Trying to keep a fire burning on twigs alone can be exhausting as you have to wander farther and farther from the fire to find fuel.

If you've been burned in the past, I encourage you to give relationships another try. Fire may be dangerous, but so is eating raw meat. God made man and woman in corresponding shapes for a reason. Our very biology tells us we weren't created to be alone. God created us for marriage, and the first command he spoke to us in the garden was to be fruitful and multiply (Genesis 1:28). You can't obey that command alone.

Gasoline may seem like an easy alternative to a carefully built fire, but throwing it on the fire will burn you. Once you add logs to the fire, you've reached sustained gasoline-level heat without the mushroom clouds and third-degree burns.

My dad likes to quote an old Jesus People saying that "the devil wants single people in bed together and married couples out of bed with each other." All you need for a healthy relationship is the diligence to build it piece by piece, step by step. A properly tended fire can burn for a lifetime.

There is a beautiful life-giving marriage out there for you. All you need to do is build it. On those cold winter nights, you'll be glad you did.

8

SEVEN ADVANTAGES OF TRADITIONAL DATING

Erica's dad taught her high school Sunday school class.

That meant he knew all the young men at her church. This was normally a good thing, except for the day he caught wind that a man named Brad was considering asking Erica out on a date. Erica's dad stood in front of the group just after the morning prayer and singled Brad out.

"Brad, I hear you're interested in asking a certain young woman out to dinner this week?"

Erica sunk into the chair as her dad's voice boomed across the room.

"Uh ... uh ... maybe." Brad's face flushed red. "Sir?"

"It sounds nice. Just make the dinner reservation for three, and don't make it too far from my house. I don't like to drive very far."

Heat rose to Erica's face. Brad opened and closed his mouth several times, stifled by Erica's father's remarks.

"I'm kidding, young man. I'd be honored for you to take my daughter out to dinner. In fact, I think every young man in this place should consider asking one of the women out this week. There are some beautiful, kind, and loving women in here. I think you'd all have a lot of fun."

Brad smiled. Erica's cheeks cooled. And a few days later, Brad called Erica and asked her to go out to a local music festival to listen to a traditional orchestra.

Some of you reading this may be shocked that this happened in a church setting, but Erica says that's the way things happened in both her church and her community. They didn't call it Traditional Dating when she was growing up, but that's exactly what they practiced in her small town. Their church had multiple guy-ask-girl dances every year, where everyone got together to dance.

On Friday nights, the guys dragged old couches down to the high school football stadium and set them up in the end zone. Then they'd invite their date of the week to watch the game from their custom-built bleachers. And on Saturdays, different couples ventured all around Erica's small town doing everything from biking to having ice cream.

Erica guesses she went on as many as fifty dates before she graduated from high school, yet she never went steady with anyone. Sure, she went out with some of the same guys multiple times, but none ever got serious. And none of her dating relationships ever involved an emotionally traumatizing breakup or a physically compromising situation.

In Erica's community, no strict ritual full of "guard your heart" rules governed dating, and the community lacked a promiscuous "hookup and breakup" culture. Because of this, most hearts were guarded and most promiscuity disappeared naturally.

Erica says that all of her close friends growing up, as well as her siblings, are now happily married. *All of them.* I can't think of a single Modern Courtship community that could say the same.

When Erica got to college, she met a man named Chris in front of the cereal bar in the cafeteria. Romantic, I know.

They talked over Lucky Charms, and that weekend they decided to go to the school football game together.

They studied in the school coffee shop the next week and ordered pizza in the dorm commons the next. Within a few months, Erica knew Chris was the kind of guy she wanted to be with. She knew that he was a good match because she'd dated so many guys before. She knew how a man should treat her. And she knew what to expect on a date.

They took it slow, spending a lot of time together as each of them worked to finish their degrees and participate in all that college had to offer. They saw each other often, but they also worked hard to build their individual lives. Erica served as a Young Life mentor and studied abroad for a year. Chris played football and did a personal training internship. While their lives intermixed, they also maintained a degree of separation.

During their senior year, George Lucas announced the release of the first of three prequels to the original Star Wars trilogy. This was huge news to everyone except for Erica. She casually mentioned that she'd never seen the original Star Wars movies, and after Chris got over his initial shock, he formed a plan.

The first thing he needed to do was talk to Erica's father and ask for his blessing. Chris had gotten to know her father over the last couple of years. Nonetheless, his hands trembled as he dialed Erica's father. After a bit of chitchat, Chris got to the point.

"Could I have your blessing to marry Erica?" His voice sounded much more confident than he felt.

Silence followed. What perhaps just took a second lasted a lifetime. Finally, Erica's father spoke. "We would love to have you as part of the family! Yes, you have my blessing."

After Chris hung up, he took a few deep breaths to calm his racing heart. "This is really going to happen!"

Chris invited Erica over the next Saturday night. He and his friends had set up a makeshift movie theater in the dorm's common room. The theater had a table with flowers, root beer (Erica's favorite), and popcorn. A couch was pulled close to the screen. And (of course) a purple light-saber with a big blue bow around it leaned next to the projector.

They watched the first three Star Wars movies together, and as the Ewoks danced and the ending credits played, Chris got down on one knee and said, "Now that you've seen Star Wars—a must for any future wife of mine—I'd like to ask for your hand in marriage."

Erica said, "Yes."

When he said, "I love you," she replied, "I know."

Okay, that last part didn't actually happen. As a Star Wars initiate, she wasn't quite ready to quote the film line-for-line.

Seven months later, they both said "I do" at a beautiful wedding. They watched the Star Wars prequels together as husband and wife. They've since had three children and named them Luke, Leia, and Han.

Okay, that's not true either. They picked family names instead, but they all love Star Wars, Jar Jar Binks notwithstanding.

After fifteen years of marriage, Erica is still in love with the man she affectionately calls "my nerd." She says that her goal for her kids is that they have a similar childhood to hers. No Modern Courtship. No hookups and breakups of Modern Dating. Instead, just good old-fashioned fun from Traditional Dating.

When I started working on this book, I thought Traditional Dating had died out. It was just a theory I had learned from my grandmother. I was wrong! I've learned from Erica's story and many others that Traditional Dating is still alive and well in some communities. It's just as practical, ethical, and fun today as it was seventy years ago.

Here are seven of Traditional Dating's many advantages:

Advantage #1: Less Heartbreak

"Why should I allow you to court my daughter?" Andrea's father asked Tim. "There's no way you're good enough for her."

Tim went home despondent and cried himself to sleep. What was so terrible about him that he couldn't even get permission to ask a girl to coffee?

He had no idea that Andrea was crying herself to sleep too.

Her father felt he was protecting "Daddy's little princess." In his eyes, she was perfect, and no imperfect young man was good enough for her. He didn't realize that he'd locked her away in a tower of unrealistic expectations that he protected like a dragon guarding its hoard.

Andrea didn't feel like a princess. She felt ugly and unwanted. She had no idea that Tim was the *fifth* young man her father had chased off in the last year. She had no idea she'd caught the attention of half the young men at her church.

> When every interaction is "for the purpose of marriage," breakups are as painful as calling off engagements.

Modern Courtship promises to lead to less heartbreak than dating. I laugh at this to keep myself from crying. When every interaction is "for the purpose of marriage," breakups are as painful as calling off engagements. Young people are left to feel alone and unlovable.

Recovery from a "failed courtship" can take years. From all over the country, I've received stories of young people whose hearts were shredded because a system promised to protect them from giving their hearts away to people they wouldn't marry.

A second hidden form of heartbreak lurks within Modern Courtship. Consider the emotional pain for women who aren't being asked out year after year. Andrea isn't the only one who's been left hurting in Modern Courtship circles.

In fact, among "stay-at-home daughters," this may be the norm. When we surveyed young singles, "not being asked" was the number one reason women gave for why they were still single. Few men are willing to fight their way past a dragon father, and fewer succeed when they try.

> **Q&A #13**
> Should I avoid women who say, "Talk to my dad"?

A third hidden form of heartbreak is the emotional cost for guys being rejected by father after father. Modern Courtship attracts dragon fathers who tend to be both unkind and ungentle. After a few negative experiences, young men often leave the courtship community and pursue Christian young women in a community that doesn't believe in courtship.

This has led to a significant gender imbalance in the Modern Courtship world. It's not uncommon to find a courtship family whose sons married outside the community and whose daughters still sit at home, waiting for someone to fight past their fathers.

To be fair, I've received a handful of accounts of fathers who let young men down gently or who even had a positive impact on their lives. One young man told me that interacting with the girl's father was one of the best experiences in his life. However, this seems to be the exception rather than the rule.

As I said before, Traditional Dating leads to less heartbreak than Modern Courtship because the relationships are less intense at first. Most of the time you can find out if someone isn't a good match without ever going through the pain of breaking up. Also, men are more likely to ask women out on dates when they don't have to fight past a dragon father or commit to marrying them at the onset. That means fewer women cry themselves to sleep out of loneliness.

Traditional Dating produces less heartbreak than Modern Dating because taking the physical relationship out of the picture means less emotional attachment. I've heard it said that sex is like super glue connecting the hearts of two people. Tearing apart those hearts after they've been glued together is a pain Traditional Dating avoids.

I should emphasize that *less* heartbreak isn't the same as *no* heartbreak. But the longer you wait to go steady, the less likely you'll have to endure a heartbreaking breakup.

Advantage #2: Less Temptation

I have to admit I was a bit suspicious when my grandmother told me "It's harder to fall for Bob on Tuesday when you know you're going out for soda pop with Bill on Thursday." But this lack of commitment leads to less expectation and less physical temptation. And less temptation leads to less compromise.

The Modern Courtship I grew up with told me to "guard my heart." But how do you do that, exactly? Some young women I knew had walls around their hearts so high that no man could garner so much as a smile from them.

> Is wearing an emotional burka really healthy?

Is emotionally shutting yourself off from the outside world the best way to guard your heart? Is wearing an emotional burka really healthy?

Could Traditional Dating's rule of "don't go steady too soon" be a more practical and healthy way to guard your heart? I decided to put it to the test.

I set up two dates in the same week with two different young women. Both dates were fun and we had a good time. And what do you know? It really works! I felt like I had a better perspective on both women and on the relationships as a whole. Also, my heart was less drawn out and I experienced less temptation.

But less commitment leading to less temptation goes against everything our culture teaches about relationships. It can be hard to go against culture. But you don't need to take my word for it.

I challenge you to see for yourself. Sign up for an online matchmaking service and go on dates with two or three people in a week and see how it goes. If you're anything like me, you'll be shocked at how much better-guarded your heart is and how much lower the temptation is.

I have no idea how people are supposed to guard their hearts while in an exclusive relationship for the purpose of marriage. Either they're so emotionally shut down that they can't bond, or they completely give their heart to the other person. Exclusivity brings with it expectations of time, touch, talk, and commitment that are unhealthy in a relationship too soon.

Advantage #3: Less Awkwardness

Traditional Dating makes interacting with the opposite sex easier and less awkward. It's easier to interact with a young woman when you don't have to ask her father's permission. It's easier for a woman to say yes to ice cream when she knows the man has none of the sexual expectations that come with Modern Dating or the marital expectations that come with Modern Courtship.

Traditional Dating gives young men a chance to practice spending time one-on-one with a young woman in a low-pressure setting. It's hard to practice getting good at wooing a woman when you only have one shot at getting it right and failure leads to years of heartache.

Talk about pressure!

The logic here is simple: Traditional Dating gives young women the chance to practice interacting with young men one-on-one without the date itself being for "the purpose of marriage" or "for the purpose of sex."

> It's hard to practice getting good at wooing a woman when you only have one shot at getting it right and failure leads to years of heartache.

Practicing interaction with young men leads to growing more comfortable around them. Being more comfortable around them leads to less awkwardness.

Modern Dating's expectation of sex right away can be super awkward. Taking sex out of the equation reduces the awkwardness for everyone.

Advantage #4: Less Intimidation

The fear of divorce catapulted Modern Courtship into popularity. A common misconception in the courtship community is that the divorce rate in America is 50 percent. People who believe this statistic think that a wedding is like playing Russian Roulette with half the chambers loaded.

The good news is that this statistic is an urban legend. In general, it's a good idea to be suspicious of round percentages that everyone knows and that never change year after year.

In her book *The Good News About Marriage,* author Shaunti Feldhahn debunks this urban legend about divorce rates. In reality, the divorce rate in America has never been as high as 50 percent, and it has steadily dropped over the last twenty years. Most marriages are happy, most women are still married to their first husband, and among people who regularly go to church the divorce rate is *even lower* than the national average. For churchgoers the divorce rate is 20–25 percent.[1]

Unfortunately, the Modern Courtship community doesn't seem to know this. It's almost as if the whole system is built on intimidation and false information: The father cleaning his shotgun at the kitchen table. Asking for the man's résumé. Expecting the young man to know he wants to marry the woman before he asks her out. It's all intimidating. And this intimidation is celebrated with Internet memes that threaten violence to young men.

It's almost as if the system was designed to scare singles away from marriage.

For many courtship-minded women to discover why they are still single, they need look no further than their father. He may have been chasing guys off for years without letting her know or giving her any say in the matter.

With Traditional Dating, asking a girl out on a date is no big deal. There's no interrogation. No shotgun. No death threats. When a guy asks a girl out for coffee, all he's asking is to get to know the girl better. He is not secretly asking to have sex with her or to marry her.

> Making a date "just a date" and not a quasi-wedding proposal makes everything less intimidating.

Maybe coffee leads to a deeper relationship, or maybe it doesn't. Making a date "just a date" and not a quasi-wedding proposal makes everything less intimidating. Dates are less intimidating and more fun when they're less intense.

Advantage #5: More Matchmaking

I know that for some of you, the music from *The Fiddler on the Roof* is already playing in your head. Sorry for hijacking your inner iPod. I'll admit I cringe a little when I hear the song "Matchmaker, Matchmaker Make Me a Match," but not all matchmaking is so final or awkward.

Rebecca is twenty-two years old and lives with her family outside a small town with one traffic light, one gas station, and a Dairy Queen. There are two other young men in her small church, but she's as uninterested in them as they are in her.

Rebecca works as a nanny for a local family, so the only single guys she meets through work still wear diapers. She dreams that Prince Charming will ask her father permission to court her. But she secretly wonders how Prince Charming will know she exists.

Most couples meet either at school, church, or work. Since Rebecca isn't in school, works as a nanny, and goes to a small church, none of these are viable options. What's more, Rebecca's Modern Courtship-minded family frowns upon online matchmaking sites since none of them have a way for her father to pre-approve suitors. So she's stuck in a world with no single men.

> So she's stuck in a world with no single men.

Modern Courtship doesn't really have a mechanism for matchmaking. Courtship relationships are so intense that even simple introductions from friends can be awkward. How can blind dates happen if the man must first get permission from a father?

Matchmaking is a time-tested practice that has occurred in multiple forms throughout the ages. Even using computers as matchmakers goes back over fifty years. There's an episode of *The Andy Griffith Show* titled "A Girl for Goober" where Goober uses a computer matchmaking service to find a date.

Modern Dating's focus on sex makes blind dates prohibitively awkward. Consequently, blind dates have dropped in popularity across the board. Not long ago, many couples met through blind dates set up by mutual friends. Ask married couples at your church who are over fifty. You might be surprised how many of them met on a blind date through a mutual friend.

If Rebecca switches to Traditional Dating, a whole world of opportunities to meet single men will open up. It'll be less awkward for her friends to make introductions. She can use online matchmaking sites, and she can even go on blind dates set up by her friends and family. She'll also have a safe place to build her confidence interacting with single men.

Advantage #6: More Fun and Romantic

Pastors around the country are bemoaning the fact that the institution of marriage is crumbling. A smaller percentage of people are married in America than at any other recorded time. This has less to do with divorce (remember that divorce rates are dropping) than it has to do with the fact many singles can't or won't get married.

A friend of mine in India once sent me a message saying, "I'm getting married next week! I'm so excited!"

"That's great! Congratulations!" I replied. "How did you meet your fiancé?"

"I will meet her this Saturday."

I raised my eyebrows. *Well, that escalated quickly.*

Cultures that practice Arranged Marriage perpetuate the institution by making marriage easy. In India, if you want to get married, just tell your parents you're ready, and they'll take care of the rest. A few months later, you begin your honeymoon.

Part of what helped perpetuate the institution of marriage in the Western world was making the process of getting married fun. When my grandmother talks about Traditional Dating, she does it with a twinkle in her eye. Those are fond memories for her.

She had a blast going on bike rides to the soda fountain with young men. She loved being wooed by my grandfather as they went steady. Ask your grandparents about Traditional Dating and I suspect you'll see this same twinkle. Traditional Dating is fun!

Traditional Dating is far more romantic than Modern Dating where you swipe right for sex with a stranger. There is no wooing in those kinds of interactions. Modern Dating may be fun in that "fleeting pleasures of sin" kind of way (Hebrews 11:25) but it leaves a hollowness and pain in its wake.

Modern Courtship, on the other hand, is more awkward than fun. I was shocked to hear from married couples who said, "We wouldn't wish our courtship experience on anyone." They act as if they survived walking through a war zone.

After hearing their stories, I want to give the husbands T-shirts that say, "I survived a Dragon Father encounter."

There's nothing wrong with having fun. Here's some advice from Solomon: "Young people, it's wonderful to be young! Enjoy every minute of it. Do everything you want to do; take it all in. But remember that you must give an account to God for everything you do" (Ecclesiastes 11:9).

What's more, there's no reason for the fun of dating to end once you say, "I do." Married couples need to continue to have fun with each other. Going on dates together is a great way to establish that habit.

So have fun! Just don't forget God in the process.

#CourtshipInCrisis

Advantage #7: More Marriage

Let's face it: Most married people got married because they dated first. Modern Courtship just isn't resulting in many marriages, despite conservative leaders advocating it for nearly twenty years.

Each of the advantages in this chapter (less heartbreak, less temptation, less awkwardness, and less intimidation) helps singles overcome obstacles to getting married and leads to more marriages. More singles will walk the path to marriage when the process of finding the love of their lives is more fun, more romantic, and easier.

The more you enjoy the journey, the less you want to give up along the way.

Traditional Dating helps people find a good match and then fall in love. It exists to help singles find the love of their lives. So while a date is just a date, both folks understand that they want to get married at some point. Perhaps it'll be the cute guy across the table. Perhaps not.

> The more you enjoy the journey, the less you want to give up along the way.

After World War II, the United States experienced a huge surge of eligible bachelors. Traditional Dating helped most of them get married in just a year or two, and that created a huge wedding boom in the late 1940s.

Today, we have a higher percentage of unmarried young people than we did after WWII, yet the wedding rates are lower than they've ever been. Singles want to get married but can't. Perhaps getting back to the system that created the wedding boom in the 1940s could create a wedding boom today.

Why Not Give Traditional Dating a Try?

Modern Courtship hasn't worked. Even the staunchest courtship advocates will admit they know a lot of unnecessarily single people in their church. And Modern Dating's hookup-and-breakup culture has led to all sorts of horrible heartbreak and pain.

When we choose between two bad options, we always make the wrong choice. So why not work up the courage to try something new?

Q&A #14: How do I switch to a Traditional Dating mindset?

Give Traditional Dating a chance to help you find the love you've been praying for.

#CourtshipInCrisis

PART 3

FINAL THOUGHTS

9

HOW TO FIND YOUR COURAGE

Fifteen steps changed everything.

My friend Alicia remembers sitting in her church's young-adult group. She observed her friends as they interacted with one another, and after several minutes of contemplation, she realized that every girl in the room was sitting in the front. Every guy in the room was sitting in the back corner.

There had been no marriages in her church for several years, and Alicia had an idea why. She thought, *No one is ever going to get married if this keeps up! But I want to get married. So this isn't going to be me.*

That night, she called a few of her girlfriends and said, "We need to sit in the guys' section of the young-adult service next week. And we need to spread out." This was a big step. In her community, many of the girls felt that if they so much as made eye contact with a single man they might "defraud" him.

It meant the girls were making an effort to show the guys that they were interested, and that was taboo.

Alicia was the first one to show up, and she boldly walked to the guys' side and sat down. Soon after that, young men started filling in the pews around her.

A few minutes later, she realized that none of her girl-friends had showed up. They had all chickened out! So she sat there awkwardly in the guys' section while the other girls in the young-adult group stared at her like, *I cannot believe the nerve of that girl ... sitting with the men!*

She'd broken an unwritten rule of her community. If only her friends had come to back her up ... but no, she was the only one. As the music played, she sat there, mortified.

The men in her young-adult service didn't seem to mind, though. After the service, the men who sat around her included her in their conversations. They asked her questions. And by the end of the night, she'd made several new friends.

At a church potluck a few days later, she sat at a table by herself. Soon afterward, seven young men joined her. Why did they give her so much attention when they had all ignored her before?

Growing up, Alicia was taught that if a girl talked to, or even *looked* at a guy, everyone would think she was flirting. Since flirting was "defrauding" and a terrible sin, the girls avoided guys altogether. They didn't want to be considered flirts.

When women ignore men to that degree, they send an unspoken signal to "get lost." When Alicia took those fifteen steps to the guys' section and talked to them, she gave them hope that they had a chance with her. In fact, she was the only girl in church they felt they had a chance with, since all the other young women kept giving off strong "get lost" vibes.

> Before a man can pursue a woman, he first has to notice her.

It was in that young-adult service that Alicia realized she

had to at least look at a guy, smile at him, and (*gasp*) talk to him before he'd pursue her. Before a man can pursue a woman, he first has to notice her.

She took those fifteen small steps. She sat on the other side. She said hello. She found something to talk about. And she let God take it from there. Today she is happily married.

Where Are All the Good Men?

"Men are cowards. Why are they so afraid to ask girls out?" Natalie stirred her coffee and shook her head. "Guys are like parking spaces. All the good ones are taken."

The funny thing about her statement is that I'd talked with a man who went to her church who felt the same way.

"Women in my church are so bound up in fear that they won't say yes to a date unless they already like you," he said. "But they won't let you near enough to get to know them. Women are like parking spaces. All the good ones are taken."

Are all the great guys taken? Are there really *no* amazing single women left? Could it be that the problem is that our perceptions are shaped by our confidence?

In some ways, the world reflects back to us what we're feeling. When we're happy, we tend to notice things that make us happy. When we're sad, it's easy to focus on the bad news.

One of the best things about writing this book is that I've had the opportunity to hear the stories of wonderful single men and women around the world. I've talked to strong, humble men who exude their passion for God. I've also talked with fantastic, beautiful women who epitomize Proverbs 31 with their God-given kindness and inner beauty.

The problem isn't that there aren't any good ones left. If we believe the statistics on how few people are getting married, then most of the good ones are still around. The problem is that they aren't connecting on a level that allows for marriage.

I think that problem comes down to fear. We are facing a confidence crisis.

Why Men Feel Undateable

Relationships require a lot of courage, particularly for men who typically take the initial risk. That begs the question: how do you become confident enough to ask a girl out? I can tell you where confidence doesn't come from: it doesn't come from giving trophies to losers. I think the self-confidence move-ment has it wrong on this point.

> Real confidence comes from past success, not from empty flattery.

When I was eight years old, I played Little League baseball. The league had a rule at our age range that no one was allowed to keep score. The scoreboards were turned off when we played, be-cause our moms didn't want us to feel bad about losing. But we all kept score in our heads. We weren't fooled by their attempt to confuse success and failure.

Real confidence comes from past success, not from emp-ty flattery. Success without the possibility of failure is like food without flavor: it has all the substance but none of the enjoyment.

Modern Courtship proponents prohibit young men from spending one-on-one time with young women and then are *shocked* when these young men become adults and lack the confidence or competence to pursue single women.

This is like prohibiting football players from playing in high school and then wondering why they're bad in col-lege. Players in college hit a lot harder. To play at that level, you need the kind of confidence and competence that comes only from years of practice.

That's one of the beautiful things about Traditional Dating. By encouraging young people to go on platonic dates while discouraging them from going steady, we give them a chance to build their confidence and competence. Wooing a woman takes practice. Getting past the cooties stage of girl-guy relationships takes time.

> Getting past the cooties stage of girl-guy relationships takes time.

Some mothers do all they can to protect their sons from failure, but later they're often surprised to see that all their sons want to do is play video games. I think the chance of failure is part of why video games appeal to young men so much. When you fail in a video game, the game rubs the failure in your face. Often you see your body on the ground while the screen pans around it with the text *"You lose!"* (or something similar) flashing in big letters.

But when the game says, *"You win,"* the message means something because failure is a real option. By protecting their children from failure in the real world, parents have banished the feeling of true success to the virtual world. The result is that success feels more real in the game than in the real world. Is it any wonder that these young men want to stay in the only world where success is an option?

If a guy asks a girl out for ice cream, it boosts the girl's confidence. If the girl says yes, the guy's confidence rises. When some girls say no, the yeses get even more meaning.

Why Women Feel Unwanted

Men aren't the only ones facing a confidence crisis. While every woman is unique, there are some things that many women have in common. For instance, many women need to know that they're beautiful.

When a woman goes a long time without hearing how pretty she is, she can think she's unattractive. The less attractive a woman feels, the less she smiles and the less she takes care of herself. This can create a vicious cycle that becomes a self-fulfilling prophecy, since men are typically more attracted to women who smile and take care of themselves.

> Ultimately we find our confidence in God, and God uses humans to encourage us.

Ultimately we find our confidence in God, and God uses humans to encourage us. We all need encouragement from others.

In many courtship communities, men don't feel like they can compliment women because that would be considered flirting—strictly taboo. The thinking is that for a man to compliment a woman, he must first be committed to marry her. So most feedback that women get on their appearance comes from other women.

Men and women don't find the same things attractive. In my experience, women have a fairly narrow view of what they consider beautiful in other women. Depending on the community, this standard can be unhealthily high and impossible to live up to.

Men, on the other hand, have a predisposition to find women attractive. I think God put this in the male psyche to help propagate our species. Furthermore, each man has a certain "type" of woman that he finds most attractive and that "type" varies from man to man.

The good news for women is that most young men find most young women attractive. I agree with the old Southern saying that "there's a lid for every pot," although I think it's fair to say that some lids fit more pots than others.

When it comes to confidence, Modern Courtship puts women at a disadvantage. Who do you think will be more confident: The woman locked in a tower, waiting for Prince Charming to fight his way past her Dragon Father? Or the woman who leaves the castle for frequent dates with a variety of princes who give her encouragement?

> The good news for women is that most young men find most young women attractive.

Having interviewed a lot of courtship-minded women, I can tell you that many of them don't feel beautiful. They're trapped in a system that isolates them from any form of encouragement or "flirting" from guys. The feedback they get from their families may also make them feel unworthy of attention.

A lot of conservatives blame "that ugly feeling" on the media. Indeed, the media has an unreasonable standard for beauty. At the end of all the makeup and Photoshop, even the models themselves can't live up to their own pictures.

But I don't think media is fully to blame for why women feel unattractive. A woman who feels loved and cherished rarely feels ugly. The same is true for the woman who is being pursued by several men. The pursued woman is less vulnerable to the media's influence. It is the lonely woman who is tempted to despair after looking at the media's impossible standard for beauty.

We can't do much about the messages the media puts out. But we *can* create a culture that is more encouraging to young women.

Single women get verbal affirmation more frequently in Traditional Dating than in Modern Courtship. The platonic, low-commitment dates of Traditional Dating give young women frequent opportunities to dress up and feel beautiful. Subsequent verbal encouragement from the young man on the other side of the table helps boost her confidence.

I should point out here that men also need verbal encouragement. Women also gain confidence from past success. While each person is unique, I don't know anyone who draws confidence from insults, failure, or constant silence.

The Confidence Crisis

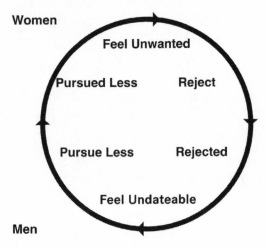

Our insecurities can form a vicious cycle. When men don't pursue women, women tend to feel ugly and unwanted. A woman who feels unwanted is more likely to hide and more likely to reject men, because the men's words sound insincere in her ears. "How could he really like me? He must be lying." So they reject men, and that makes men feel less confident. In turn, that makes men less likely to pursue women, and so the cycle continues.

Courtship encourages singles to "spend time in groups" without realizing that most group interactions are gender-segregated. There are few girls at the game night and few men at the prayer meeting. A wedge of insecurity seems to separate the men from the women.

The joke in my area is that you know you're at a "homeschool party" when the guys and girls chat in mostly separate groups. Even at gatherings of college graduates, when the sexes start to cluster, someone asks, "Is this a homeschool party?"

> God is bigger than our failures, rejections, temptations, and divorces.

Fear has saturated the Modern Courtship community:

* Fear of failure
* Fear of divorce
* Fear of temptation
* Fear of rejection

The fear can choke us so much that it's hard to breathe, much less thrive. The parents are afraid. The pastors are afraid. The singles are afraid.

I have some good news:

In the words of an old VeggieTales song: "God is bigger than the boogie man." God is bigger than our failures, rejections, temptations, and divorces. He has provided a way out of the confidence crisis. God didn't give us a spirit of fear (2 Timothy 1:7). He doesn't want us to be afraid.

Seven Steps to Find Your Courage

No one is born courageous. Most babies cry at loud noises, and most children are afraid of the dark. But anyone can find courage. There are few things more powerful in this world than someone who, while facing fear, chooses to act anyway.

Here are seven steps to help you become a more courageous person.

#CourtshipInCrisis

Step 1: Be Afraid

Boldness is the absence of fear. You either have it or you don't. The best way to be bold is to be ignorant of the risk.

Courage, on the other hand, is action in the face of fear. Courage is doing the right thing despite possessing a vivid understanding of the danger. So the first step to finding courage is identifying the fear. Without fear you cannot show courage.

Fear is like Red Bull. It focuses the mind, heightens the senses, and boosts energy. Courage redirects that energy and points it in a positive direction.

> As my speech coach told me, "Good public speaking isn't about getting rid of the butterflies. It's about getting them to fly in formation."

As a professional public speaker, I learned that my best talks happened when I was terrified. As my speech coach told me, "Good public speaking isn't about getting rid of the butterflies. It's about getting them to fly in formation." There's a level of energy I can achieve onstage only when I'm jittery with fear.

What do you fear? Does the idea of asking that cute girl at church out for ice cream make you want to vomit? Does the thought of spending time alone with a guy at a coffee shop tempt you to run away and hide? Are you terrified of repeating the painful mistakes of your past?

These fears intend to cripple you into inaction, but they don't have to. They can instead empower you to do something you would otherwise never be able to do. But the first step is to acknowledge the fear and see it as separate from who you are. Just naming the fear can start to lift its hold over you. As my pastor Geno Hildebrandt says, "Name the fear, call it what it is, and then say to yourself, '*I am not the sum of my fear*.'"

This really does work, but you don't have to take my word for it. Try it yourself and see if your courage increases.

Step 2: Find Out Who You Are

If you're a follower of Christ, you've received a new identity (2 Corinthians 5:17), and you're now a child of light (Ephesians 5:8). You're born again as a son or daughter of the King of Kings (Romans 8:15–16). God has given you a new name (Revelation 2:17). He has taken your garments of wickedness and replaced them with robes of righteousness (Galatians 3:26–27).

You are *not* a coward. The Bible tells us, "The wicked flee when no one pursues, but the righteous are bold as a lion" (Proverbs 28:1 ESV).

Knowing who you are in Christ can change how you see your fear. Yes, a heavenly perspective on your problems can make them look small in light of the universe, but this is more than that. True confidence can't come from others. It comes only from God.

> True confidence can't come from others. It comes only from God.

We find a good example of the power of identity in the book of Judges. For years the Midianites had attacked the Israelites. They were so cruel that the Israelites hid in caves anytime the Midianites came around. The worst part was that the Midianites took all the food they could get their hands on. What they didn't take, they burned, causing a famine across the land.

But God chose to intervene. He sent an angel to speak to a man named Gideon, who was hiding at the bottom of a winepress. What did the angel say to this man? Did he say,

"Climb out of that winepress, you coward. God wants you to save Israel"?

No. He said, "Mighty hero, the Lord is with you!" (Judges 6:12). The first thing the angel gave to Gideon was a new identity. He was no longer Gideon the coward hiding in a hole. He was Gideon the mighty hero.

Once Gideon received his new identity, he left the winepress, because mighty heroes don't hide in holes. Gideon went on to have a series of adventures, culminating in a surprise attack where he and three hundred men ambushed the Midianite army.

> Many of us learned to guard against pride by putting ourselves down. But this isn't true humility.

God blessed Gideon's courage and caused the massive enemy army to fight itself in panic. Gideon rescued Israel and led it into a season of peace and prosperity. At the risk of sounding like Chris from *Adventures in Odyssey*, you can read about the rest of Gideon's adventures in Judges 6–8.

Ask God to tell you who you are. As He gives you a new identity, don't be surprised when your courage starts to grow.

Step 3: Change Your Self-Talk

When it comes to finding our confidence, we are often our own worst enemies. What do you tell yourself when you look in the mirror? Is it words of encouragement and affirmation? If you're like me, you're much meaner to yourself than you are to anyone else.

Many of us learned to guard against pride by putting ourselves down. But this isn't true humility. It has been said, "True humility is not thinking less of yourself. It is thinking of yourself less."[1] False humility (rejecting compliments, dismissing strengths, and emphasizing weaknesses) can actually be symptoms of pride.

For example, when we reject someone's compliment, we're saying, "My view of me is more important than your view of me." That's an arrogant way to be humble.

If anyone doled out as much verbal abuse to one of my family members as I do to myself, I wouldn't tolerate it. I'd fight to defend my family from anyone who talked to them that way, yet I put up with my own terrible self-talk.

People who hate themselves tend to judge others more harshly. The meaner I am to myself, the meaner I tend to be toward others. It's hard to love my neighbor as myself when I treat myself so badly.

In 2 Corinthians 10:5, the apostle Paul talks about taking our thoughts captive and forcing them to be obedient to Christ. This idea that we have control over our own thoughts is a powerful principle.

> It's hard to love my neighbor as myself when I treat myself so badly.

Deciding in your mind that you believe what God says about you more than what you think about yourself could be called "repentance." Repentance literally means to change your thinking, but changing your thinking can be harder than changing your actions. I can believe what God says about others, but can I believe what He says about me?

Gideon had to change his thinking when the angel called him a mighty hero while he was still hiding. He had to repent from thinking of himself as a coward. This change in his self-talk required faith.

His faith started very small. He didn't go straight from hiding to ambushing the Midianite army. He had a series of adventures first. Each adventure helped grow his faith. God patiently helped Gideon adjust to his new identity.

There's a powerful moment in *The Lord of the Rings* when the Fellowship is being chased by a giant fire demon called a Balrog. Finally, Gandalf, the leader of the party, turns around and faces the monster.

What happens next is one of my favorite passages in the book:

> "You cannot pass," he said. The orcs stood still, and a dead silence fell. "I am a servant of the Secret Fire, wielder of the flame of Anor. You cannot pass. The dark fire will not avail you, flame of Udûn. Go back to the Shadow! You cannot pass." [2]

Gandalf knew exactly what he was facing. He had every reason to be afraid. But he also knew who he was. He spoke his identity to himself as much as to the monster. He had the courage to face the monster and save his friends.

Step 4: Suit Up

On the football field, wearing pads and a helmet gives the players courage. But perhaps more importantly, they're also wearing a uniform. The uniform says, "I'm on a team. The other guys in this uniform have my back. Together we're going to do what none of us could do alone." Often unnoticed on ESPN highlight reels is the rest of the team helping to make a big play possible.

As Christians, God clothes us in robes of righteousness and places us on His team, the Body of Christ. In a spiritual sense, we suit up when we put on our uniform and embrace our role within the Body. God not only surrounds us with fellow warriors, but he also gives us heavenly pads and a helmet to keep us safe (Ephesians 6:10–18).

Surrounding yourself with fellow believers who encourage and look out for you can boost your confidence. You could say that when Jesus talked about the "Friend of the Bridegroom" (John 3:29 ESV), he was talking about what we today would call a wingman. If you're shy, having a good friend who can act as a wingman to make introductions for you can be very helpful.

In one sense, John the Baptist was Jesus's wingman. He helped introduce people to Jesus. The key to being a good wingman (or wingwoman) is to know how to gracefully leave the conversation once things get started. There comes a moment in these conversations when the wingmate must decrease so the friend can increase.

We can also suit up in a literal sense. There's an ancient Latin saying: *Vestus virum reddit*—the clothes make the man. How you dress signals your body how to act.

I saw this firsthand in speech and debate. It amazed me how young men behaved differently when they wore a suit and tie. If you want to get in the mood for exercise, put on your exercise clothes. Somehow your clothes can change your mood.

Clothes are a tangible way to signal both to yourself and to others what you think about yourself. If you see yourself as a slob, you'll dress like a slob. If you see yourself as an attractive and confident person, your clothes will reflect that.

Suiting up isn't just about clothing, it's about how you carry yourself.

Stand tall. Roll your shoulders back. Look the world in the face with a smile. You may be surprised to find the world smiling back at you. Lift your chin and let confidence flow through you.

You're not a beggar who keeps his eyes on the ground. You're a child of God. The more you act like it, the more you'll feel it.

Step 5: Take Risks

The first time I sang in a choir, I shook with nerves. Sweat dripped from my forehead and I could hardly get the words out. Years later, I could sing confidently without a hint of nerves.

What changed?

I sang in over a hundred choir performances. I took risks by auditioning. That practice and those risks gave me confidence to try bigger challenges in the future. What intimidated me as a child no longer scared me as a teen.

When my family started the Austin Rhetoric Club, we found that a lot of students would join the club only to leave before delivering a single speech. So we changed the rules. Everyone gave a speech their first day at the club, even if it was just to introduce themselves. The first speech always proved the hardest, but once students got it out of the way, coming back became a lot easier.

> The longer we put off dating, the scarier it becomes.

When students put off that first speech, it grew into a monster in their minds. They wanted more and more training before they felt ready to give the speech. The more training they received, the more they realized they didn't know, until they finally just gave up and stopped coming.

Some things can be learned only by doing. You can't learn how to play the violin from a book. The only way to learn how to play the violin well is to first play poorly.

Interacting with the opposite sex is the same way. We're tempted to believe that the longer we wait, the easier it will be. This is like putting off violin practice in hope that we will play better by procrastinating instead of practicing.

Likewise, the longer we put off dating, the scarier it becomes. So we grab another relationship book and hope to get more ready. Books aren't a replacement for practice. The sooner you work through the awkwardness of cooties, the sooner you can find your confidence.

I say this as someone who still struggles with this specific fear. When I first started Traditional Dating, I got so nervous I couldn't eat. I was so soaked with nervous sweat at the end of one date that the girl told me she didn't want to go out again because of how I smelled.

> **Q&A #15**
> I want to try Traditional Dating, but all of my friends are courtship-minded. What should I do?

Just the thought of going on a date made my heart race. Excuses for why I should cancel flew through my mind. But I've learned that sometimes I have to take action while I'm scared. If I wait for the fear to go away, I'll wait a lifetime. So I bought a stronger antiperspirant and tried again.

I've learned through hard experience that the more I ask girls out, the easier it becomes. The longer I put it off, the more of a monster it becomes in my mind. So if you're a guy, ask a girl out for lunch. It won't get easier by waiting.

Women, if the guy's a Christian and he asks you to dinner, say yes. If you don't know him very well, drive yourself so you can leave without him if you feel uncomfortable. But give him a chance. Who knows? You might even have fun!

Step 6: Fail and Try Again

When I was thirteen, my family rented a WaveRunner for our family reunion at the beach. I rode behind my older cousin and we hit a massive wave. I launched into the air and hit the water hard.

Then my legs caught on fire. In the water.

"Take me back to the beach!" I gasped. Hundreds of hot

needles stabbed my legs again and again, and the pain refused to subside. It was getting worse.

Once we got to the beach, I saw that I'd landed on top of a Portuguese man-of-war. Venomous tentacles had curled up and down my legs and even into my swimsuit. It hurt so bad that I cried (which, for a thirteen-year-old boy, was mortifying).

A line of cousins stood nearby, waiting their turn to ride the WaveRunner, and all I wanted to do was go back to the condo and hide. As I started to slink away, I felt a hand on my shoulder. It was my Uncle Bobby.

"Thomas," he said with a kind smile, "if you go back home now, you may always be afraid of going out in those waves. You need to get back on the horse that threw you. If you want to go again, you can cut the line. The best thing for you is to get back in the ocean. The salt water will help you heal."

"Okay." I wiped away my tears and tried to look brave.

The last thing I wanted was to get back in the ocean. That was a place of pain, not a place of healing. I slinked off to a nearby sandcastle and watched as my cousins took turns on the WaveRunner. *It's not fair that they're having so much fun when my legs are on fire,* I thought as I doused my burning legs with a plastic bucket of salt water.

> There's a kind of courage that's only forged through failure.

Finally, I walked back to the line. *I'll just stand in line,* I told myself. When the WaveRunner got back, all my cousins looked at me, silently asking if I wanted the next ride.

Now I felt like I *had* to go. To save face, I took the next ride. We took it slow, and I didn't fall off again.

As we coasted back to the beach, my fear of the ocean, WaveRunners, and evil, stinging man-of-wars dissipated in our wake. My legs still hurt, but the weight of fear on my shoulders lifted. I felt so free. Each time I waded back into the salt water, the pain in my legs diminished even more.

For some of us, our experience with romance has felt like falling onto a Portuguese man-of-war—or worse. We're tempted to say, "I'm never doing this again. I'll be single the rest of my life. At least that way I won't have to experience this excruciating pain again."

If that's you, I'd like to encourage you to give it another try. Going back to that place of pain and trying again may be the only way to find true healing. Salt water really is the best treatment for man-of-war venom.

There's a kind of courage that's only forged through failure. Someone who has never failed has never found the limit of his or her abilities. They're too timid to take risks but are likely far more capable than they realize.

If we never fail, the fear of failure can grow like a splinter in our minds, driving us deeper into darkness. A man who has never experienced failure can only imagine how it feels to fail. It's easy for his imagination to run away with him.

Failure doesn't build confidence. Overcoming failure builds confidence. So to overcome failure you must first fail.

> You never truly know God loves you when you fail, until you fail and experience God's love.

Failure is like hot coffee. It's too hot to touch, but not too hot to drink. Once you learn to drink the heat of failure, it loses its power over you. If all you do is touch the hot coffee with your finger, you'll start to believe it's undrinkable. But you gain a special kind of confidence when you can say, "I survived. I'm still here. I can do this."

Failure can also bring you closer to God. You never truly know God loves you when you fail, until you fail and experience God's love. Once you experience the love of God in the midst of your failure, nothing can stop you.

> And I am convinced that nothing can ever separate us from God's love. Neither death nor life, neither angels nor demons, neither our fears for today nor our worries about tomorrow—not even the powers of hell can separate us from God's love.
>
> Romans 8:38

Often the place of our greatest pain is also the source of God's greatest healing. The deep places of our pain cry out to the deep places of God's love. But the depths of His love extend far deeper than the depths of our pain. Once God's love pours into us, we grow stronger than we were before the failure, and we become more confident in taking risks.

Step 7: Experience God's Love

The Bible tells us in 1 John 4:18 that "Such love has no fear, because perfect love expels all fear." While it's true that a mother will put herself in harm's way to save her child, there's more to this verse than that. God's perfect love for us casts out our fear.

Do you feel deep down that God loves you? He loves you so much that He sent His Son to die so that you could be reconciled to Him. He loves you so much that He gave His Holy Spirit to guide you in your daily life.

> A man with an experience is not at the mercy of a man with an argument.

You can experience God's love for you. There's an old saying that a man with an experience is not at the mercy of a man with an argument. Once you personally experience the love of God, you'll never be the same.

God wants to shower you in love in such a way that you can experience it. All you have to do is ask Him.

From Vicious Cycle to Virtuous Cycle

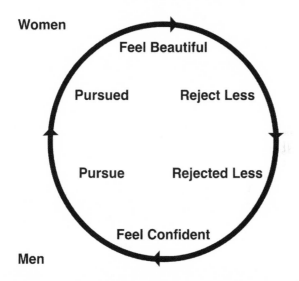

As men overcome their fear and pursue women, women will feel more beautiful, which will make them less likely to reject the men around them. This will encourage more men to pursue them and the positive cycle continues.

All it takes to start the change is a simple compliment, an invitation to coffee, or a yes to lunch. You can do it!

10

QUESTIONS & ANSWERS

Since my blog post "Why Courtship is Fundamentally Flawed" came out last year, I've received thousands of questions and comments from all over the world. This chapter has synthesized versions of some of those questions. Single letters are swapped for people's names.

If you have a question or comment for a future version of this book, feel free to drop me a line at www.ThomasUmstattd.com.

Question #1: I've never been asked out on a date. I want to get married. What should I do?

Dear Thomas,

I'm a 25-year-old single woman. I graduated from college three years ago and moved back home to save money. I have a great job and great friends and a fairly active social life. I go to our church's singles' group on Thursday nights and have coffee with my girlfriends on Wednesday mornings before work to talk about life. I feel like I live a fairly well-rounded and well-adapted life.

But there's one thing: I have never once been asked out on a date. Not once in high school, not once in college, and not once since I moved back in with my parents. I've prayed so fervently and trusted God to move in this area of my life for so long but all to no avail. I'm honestly starting to get discouraged. I want to get married and have children, but as time moves on, it seems more and more like an impossible dream.

Please help!

Sincerely,
S

Dear S,

As a man, I hesitated to answer this question, but after hearing similar questions from dozens of women, I need to make an attempt. I asked several married women, as well as some single men, to weigh in, and we came up with six tips to help you out.

Tip #1: Ask for Personal Advice

First, I'd recommend talking to a friend who is recently married, and ask her to coach you. Talk to your mom as well. Ask them lots of questions about how they found the right one, what they did as they got to know their spouse, and how they fostered the growth of their romantic relationships.

If the folks around you aren't much help, consider taking a look at the book *Not Your Mother's Rules* by Ellen Fein & Sherrie Schneider. The book speaks from a secular perspective, but it's packed full of practical and specific advice that really works. A homeschooled friend of mine went from having about one date per year to one date per week after reading *Not Your Mother's Rules*. She recommends it to anyone who will listen.

Tip #2: Take Action

Trusting God isn't an acceptable excuse for inaction. You don't sit on the couch trusting that God will do the dishes for you. Instead, you trust your God-given ability to wash the dishes yourself. God put us on this planet to work, and relationships require work from both the man and the woman. Don't confuse laziness with holiness.

An old Chinese proverb says, "He who waits for roast duck to fly into mouth must wait a very, very long time."

Tip #3: Watch Your Vibes

Girls send out a certain vibe when they're in a relationship with a man. This vibe communicates that they're "off the market." Some Christian girls unintentionally put out this vibe in an attempt to "guard their hearts." The result is that honorable men leave them alone, and they either attract dishonorable men or no men at all.

My advice to you is to be friendly to guys. Make eye contact, smile, laugh, and give them attention. I can think of nothing more attractive about a girl than a genuine smile.

Before a guy can pursue you, he first needs to notice you and have hope that he has a chance with you. This can make for a beautiful relational dance. But like any dance, this one requires both people to participate.

Tip #4: Look Your Best

If you always look like you're ready for a date, you're more likely to get asked out on a date. I don't care what Disney tells you, young men really do care about looks—Christian men included. If they cared only about godly character and maturity, there would be no old widows in the church.

I'm not aware of any teaching in the Bible that forbids women from looking beautiful. The Song of Songs is a celebration of female beauty, strange metaphors notwithstanding. Looking your best doesn't mean you have to go through twelve months of beauty treatments like Queen Esther (Esther 2:12) or look like a supermodel. Just look like your best self. It really does make a difference.

Tip #5: Move Your Purity Ring

If you wear a purity ring, move it to your non-wedding-ring hand. In America, that would be the right hand. A ring on your wedding ring finger will look like an engagement ring, and it communicates to honorable men that you're taken.

When my sister made this shift, suddenly many more honorable men started asking her out. It was a Cinderella-like change. Even as a guy, I wear my purity ring on my right hand.

Tip #6: Sign Up for an Online Matchmaking Site

Consider signing up for a few online matchmaking sites. These sites really do work and have resulted in millions of happy marriages. They can also give you practice dating, which will help you overcome dating jitters.

Finding a good husband is worth paying for, so don't be afraid of the paid-membership sites. If a man can't afford an online matchmaking site, that tells you something about his finances.

Don't give up. You can do this!

Thomas

Question #2: Is Joshua Harris to blame for the courtship crisis?

Dear Thomas,

After spending the last ten years trying to follow a model that is not only awkward but also didn't live up to its promise that it would help me find a spouse, I have to admit that I'm a little angry. I look back and wish someone had warned me that all the promises I believed would never come to fruition.

I wish I'd never heard of courtship or Joshua Harris. I can't help but feel like Joshua Harris ruined my life. Am I wrong to be so upset?

Hurt by Modern Courtship,
D

Hi D,

Ultimately, we're all responsible for our own decisions. I have no one to blame for my failures other than myself.

I hold a deep respect for Joshua Harris. His teaching helped lead millions of young people away from promiscuity. He helped move us from the cultural norm of hooking up on the first date to having a first kiss at the altar. His call for holiness is something we should heed still. I remember being so fired up for Christ after listening to one of his teachings that I shared the gospel with a couple of complete strangers at a Walgreens. I just couldn't help myself.

I really respect him for dedicating his life to advancing the Kingdom full-time by leading and planting churches. In preparation for writing *Courtship in Crisis*, I reread parts of *I Kissed Dating Goodbye*. A large part of that book is a call to make Jesus Lord, which is also the message of this book.

I know Modern Courtship has wounded many people in the past. Some of the stories I've heard have broken my heart. I had no idea how bad it was for some people. These outcomes were *not* Joshua Harris's intent. Like me, he was a single man trying to respond to a broken relationship culture, trying to direct people back to Christ.

Other religious leaders weaponized Harris's teachings and used them to chain singles into a rigid set of rules. They turned *I Kissed Dating Goodbye* into a religious system called Modern Courtship.

One of my fears is that people will do the same thing with this book. I don't want to see Traditional Dating turned into yet another set of chains. Please say no to legalism. Instead, say yes to the grace and hope of Christ.

Sincerely,

Thomas

Question #3: I courted and I am now happily married. How can you say it doesn't work?

Dear Thomas,

I have to disagree with you! My husband and I courted and we have a great relationship. We went through the entire process and have now been happily married for five years. I recommend the courtship model to my single friends on a regular basis because it worked for me. I think your assertion that courtship is fundamentally flawed is a fundamentally flawed argument.

Sincerely,
K

Dear K,

My thesis is not that Modern Courtship is *universally* flawed. It is *fundamentally* flawed in the same way the Yugo was a fundamentally flawed car. Yugos sometimes worked. For some people they lasted years. But eventually they all broke. While all cars break down eventually, some cars break down faster than others. The better the initial design, the longer the car lasts.

Many of the successful Modern Courtship stories I have

collected contain a statement like "we used a modified form of courtship." So they knew they needed to modify the Yugo to make it more reliable. If you're a good mechanic, you can keep a Yugo running longer. This does not negate the premise that the fundamental design is flawed.

I suspect most singles would prefer their romance be more like a BMW than a Yugo.

I'm not saying Modern Courtship is evil or that it will inevitably lead to singleness or divorce. God gives us a lot of freedom when it comes to relationships. If Modern Courtship worked for you, great!

> I suspect most singles would prefer their romance be more like a BMW than a Yugo.

If it's not working for someone, I humbly suggest an old-fashioned alternative called Traditional Dating, which worked for my grandparents' generation. I think it is the best fit for our culture.

That said, I should point out that Traditional Dating is not a perfect system. One of its weaknesses is for couples to stay in the dating phase and to never transition into going steady. Any system that involves people will include the imperfections of those people

Just because a system is flawed doesn't make it wrong or evil. I'm not here to judge you if you prefer Modern Courtship. I'm just here to advocate for what I believe is a more practical system.

Thank you for your feedback,

Thomas

Question #4: I courted, and now I am in an abusive relationship. What should I do?

Dear Thomas,

My husband and I have been married for two years. We courted. I can look back now and see the warning signs that things weren't good, but back then I assumed it was the awkwardness of courtship and that things would settle down once we got married. They didn't.

Looking back, I wish I'd listened to my own intuition, but by the time we were officially courting, it was too late for me to call it off. It would've been quite the scandal. So I smiled and pretended it was all okay.

Three months after we were married, we had our first fight, and he hit me. The abuse has continued, and I'm not sure where to turn. What should I do now? My parents would be furious if I got a divorce after everything they did to help me find the right spouse.

Thanks in advance,

A

Dear A,

You are a child of our heavenly Father. He loves you. You belong to Him and no one else. Don't let anyone twist the Scripture into an excuse for abuse.

There are safe places where you can go to get help. You can call the National Domestic Violence Hotline anytime at 1-800-799-SAFE or 1-800-799-7223. You can visit their website at www.thehotline.org.

If your church feels like an unsafe place, find a trustworthy friend or a family member who will shelter you until you can get further help. Whatever you do, don't stay in an abusive situation because anyone—your parents, your church, your friends—thinks you should.

Praying for you,

Thomas

Question #5: Why can't we just spend time in groups?

Dear Thomas,

My friends and I always hang out in groups. We go bowling together or to the movies or even out to ice cream. I feel like I've gotten to know several of the guys in our friendship circle pretty well this way, although I admit that I've never "courted" or "dated" any of them.

I guess it makes me wonder why hanging out in groups wouldn't work as a method to finding "the one."

Cordially,
M

Dear M,

Spending time in groups sounds great in theory. A group setting gives singles a low-pressure way to get to know one another. But they tend to break down in practice, particularly when group settings are the only approved method of interaction.

Groups Aren't Great for Working Adults

As the CEO of a tech company, I know firsthand that organizing group activities with working adults is a chore. Each person you add to the group activity exponentially increases the scheduling challenge.

Some people work office hours, some work retail hours, and some work in restaurants. Meanwhile, nurses work twelve hours a day, four days a week, and some work weekends. These are all common work schedules for young people just entering the workforce, and they're incompatible with scheduling group activities.

Two people can easily find time to meet, but if they need to invite a few working friends just to turn it into a group activity, they may not be able to find a time to meet until the next month. The result? Very few group activities actually happen.

Groups Disadvantage Rural Singles

Many practitioners of courtship live in suburban or rural areas where setting up group activities requires a lot of logistics and travel. The result for these singles is that few group activities actually happen, and when they do, they involve the same group again and again.

Groups Reduce Your Options

As you invest in relationships with a group, you tend to want to stay with that group. They're your friends, after all.

But what do you do if no one in the group is interested in you? Do you try to find other groups to join? Does that mean you have to spend less time with your friends in order to find a spouse?

Groups Disadvantage Some Personality Types

Not all personality types shine in a group setting. Singles activities are such a hassle to coordinate that when they do happen, often dozens or even hundreds of people get involved.

Some personality types tend to hide in these situations. You know the gathering is too big when the bathrooms are full of introverts hiding from the crowd. Should these shy people be doomed to a life of singleness because of their personalities?

Groups Work Best for Students

Group activities work best for students because they have coordinated schedules. No one has class at 9 PM and everyone has Sunday off. When you live in a dorm and you're surrounded by hundreds of singles within walking distance, it's easy to put together spur-of-the-moment hangout times or group study sessions. I had more group activities in one month of college than I had in a year's worth of post-college life.

With that in mind, I think one-on-one dating is better for most people.

Sincerely,

Thomas

Question #6: Are you saying parents should be uninvolved in the process like they are in Modern Dating?

Dear Thomas,

I've always really valued my parents' opinions. I've talked through with them almost every decision I've ever made, and their wisdom, guidance, and advice has greatly influenced me. I can't imagine excluding them from the process of choosing my spouse!

Are you saying that in Traditional Dating the parents should be uninvolved in the process entirely? I would hate that.

Regards,

P

Dear P,

No. No. No. Parents should definitely be involved.

It makes sense that the younger a child is, the more control the parents extend over his or her life. Bestselling author James L. Rubart has a three-step process he went through with his sons of Dictator, Coach, and Friend. As his sons matured, the nature of his relationship with them changed.

He told his two-year-old son not to go into the street "because I said so." Dictator-style parenting doesn't work for older children who occasionally need to go into the street. At some point, parents need to transition from a dictator to coaches who explain how to safely cross the street and later how to drive on that street.

By the time James's sons turned eighteen, they had transitioned into the "friend stage" with him. This sounds very healthy to me. They still seek his advice and enjoy spending time with him because they maintain a strong trust connection. But they have the final say in all of their decisions. He recognizes that they are adults.

The kind of parental involvement in Traditional Dating differs from Modern Courtship. Traditional Dating stresses the parental role as a trusted advisor rather than a dictator. The young person is making a lifetime commitment, and he or she needs to have freedom to make the best decision. The only way to do this is to practice making decisions. That means parents need to coach rather than command.

The kind of parent who feels that "no control" is "no involvement" may have control issues. If my blog comments are any gauge, most young people long for relationship advice from their parents. Relationships are scary and one way to handle that fear is to ask for lots of advice.

Parents play a vital role in Traditional Dating. If their

child is not yet an adult, they meet the dates and give their son or daughter advice on what they like and don't like about each one. This way they help their children learn to make their own good decisions.

Then both young people (if they're still minors) get permission from their own parents before they start "going steady." During the "going steady" phase, the parents continue giving advice and encouragement. If both singles are adults, this permission step is skipped, although advice is often still sought if there is trust in the parent-child relationship.

> The kind of parent who feels that "no control" is "no involvement" may have control issues.

In Traditional Dating, the man asks for permission or blessing from the girl's father before they transition from "going steady" to engagement. This step typically happens regardless of age. So a forty-year-old man would still ask for blessing before popping the question to a forty-year-old woman.

During the engagement phase, the couple still receives parental guidance. The culmination of this usually occurs at the rehearsal dinner, where the parents typically give short speeches of relationship advice and encouragement.

I hope that helps!

Thomas

Question #7: What do you think about secret courtships?

Hello Thomas,

P just asked me to be his girlfriend, and I said yes. Both our families are very excited for us. He said he doesn't want to make our relationship "Facebook Official" because that would make things weird with our church. Is it a good idea to keep our relationship secret from folks outside our family?

Sincerely,
D

Dear D,

One of the common "modifications" within Modern Courtship is for couples to keep their relationship a secret from friends until near the engagement. Couples do this because they fear their community will blow out the fire of their budding relationship with expectations, pressure, and meddling.

It's critical that communities tend these young flames in a healthy way so couples don't feel the need to hide. Otherwise couples will be tempted to keep their relationships secret, which is bad for everyone.

I encourage you to be Facebook Official with your relationship.

There are several downsides to keeping a relationship secret.

Downside #1: You Spend Less Time with Your Other Friends

It's not uncommon to see someone fade from their community as a romantic relationship starts. Modern Courtship is a relationship with the intention of marriage. Who has time for friends while developing such an intense attachment?

But you're going to need those friends.

By isolating yourself from friends, you create the expectation that your sweetheart will become your primary supply of all your emotional needs. This is an unhealthy expectation to put on one person, and it's a common source of marital conflict down the road. No one human can be your everything. If that is your expectation then disappointment is inevitable.

If a man's wife is his best and only friend, then he has a problem. The reality is that men need guy friends to be healthy. Men have relationship needs that a girlfriend/wife just can't fulfill. The same goes for women needing other women.

I think the traditional wedding ceremony is a great model for what a healthy marital relationship should look like. The groom does not have just his bride. He also has his best man. The bride has her maid of honor. Watching from the pews are their parents and friends. Standing between the couple is the minister who represents the love of our Creator.

Downside #2: You Miss Out on Community Feedback

Okay, so you think this guy is cute, and your dad gave him

permission to pursue you. But how does he interact with your friends? Do your friends like him? If not, why not? If so, how so?

When you interact only with each other and with each other's families (when you're both on your best behavior), you don't get to see the real person.

My original blog post "Why Courtship is Fundamentally Flawed" received over 1,400 comments. Included were dozens and dozens of horror stories from couples who courted only to find out later that they didn't really know the person they were courting until after they said, "I do."

The most common theme included women with abusive boyfriends who put on a front for their fathers. Then, when the father had no more say in the matter, the real version of the man showed up. Since the relationships were short and secret, these men could easily hide their inner monsters. These types of situations are where a community of friends can really help.

An abusive, controlling person can hide for a short time, but he can't hide his true nature all of the time. The longer the relationship lasts and the more friends you have in common, the more likely you are to find out if Mr. Hyde is hiding inside of Dr. Jekyll. Your friends can help save you from Mr. Hyde by giving you additional perspectives on your potential sweetheart. They can also help you know of any other deal breakers that might be hiding.

Downside #3: You Miss Out on Mediators

When a relationship hits a rough patch, which will inevitably happen, it's nice to have friends who know both of you and who can talk you off the ledge. Sometimes tears can cloud our vision, and we need a friend to help give us perspective.

You need a friend who can tell you:

"I know that's what he said, but I also know his character.

I'm sure he didn't mean it that way. Sometimes guys put their foot in their mouths and say stupid things." or "This is the third time this has happened. I know he says he will change but I know him and I just don't see that happening." or "I talked with her. She's heartbroken over what she said. You should call her back and let her explain and apologize."

> Sometimes tears can cloud our vision, and we need a friend to help give us perspective.

It's true that a couple can rely on mediators too much and fail to learn how to communicate with each other, but sometimes a neutral mediator can save a relationship.

Mediation is one area where family isn't a good option. Your family is on your side. They're your shoulders to cry on and your ears to confide in. Do you really want your family to be neutral? Because whatever happens in the relationship, they'll still be your family.

A mutual friend, on the other hand, loves you both. Good mediators take no one's side. In wanting the best for both of you, that friend can help you find common ground or help you decide it's time to move on.

Sincerely,

Thomas

Question #8: Are you saying that we can rely solely on human wisdom in relationships?"

Dear Thomas,

I really want to trust God for my future and my future marriage. It feels like if I start Traditional Dating, I'm turning my trust away from the Bible. Are you saying that we can rely solely on human wisdom in relationships?

Sincerely,

E

Dear E,

Nope.

No system is a substitute for the Holy Spirit. No system can compensate for broken people. We all need God's healing and guidance in our lives.

> Saying that we either listen to common sense or listen to God is a false dichotomy.

Saying that we either listen to common sense or listen to God is a false dichotomy. We should ignore common sense when God tells us to, and allow the peace of Christ to rule in our hearts (Colossians 3:15).

Otherwise, there is a lot of safety in the common-sense advice passed down through the generations. Thinking we are above this generational wisdom can be a form of pride.

Sincerely,

Thomas

Question #9: Is it okay to kiss?

Dear Thomas,

I come from a background where Modern Courtship was encouraged, so when I read your blog post about Traditional Dating, I thought you were nuts. But I decided to give it a try. After going on dates with several different women, I met S. The instant I met her, I knew she was different.

She's beautiful, smart, funny, and she loves Jesus. I'm smitten. We had the talk last week and decided to start going steady, and both of us are slowly but steadily walking toward marriage.

Which leads me to my question. I can't believe I'm even going to ask this considering my past views on dating and purity, but since I've done such an about-face on everything else that has to do with dating, I figure I might as well get it all out there. Would it be okay for me to kiss S?

I don't want to do anything to dishonor her or God, but I'm realizing that a lot of the values I once held true aren't actually from the Bible. What do you think?

Converted from Courtship,

B

Dear B,

I remember talking at a church to a group of parents a while back about Traditional Dating. They had a lot of questions about appropriate forms of physical contact. I didn't know what to tell them. Every family is different, and within each family, every child is different. Who am I to dictate what rule should apply in all those situations?

Then one of the moms asked me what I thought about kissing. I didn't know what to tell her. I grew up with the "nerd blessing" in that I was so awkward around girls that nothing went anywhere. In short, I'd never kissed anyone. I told her "I don't know" and went on to the next question.

When I got home I did what any good nerd would do. I studied kissing in a book. And I came up with my official position on premarital kissing.

Like you mentioned in your question, I could find no rule in Scripture against kissing. I found no eleventh commandment that said, "Thou shalt not kiss." In fact, the apostle Paul says repeatedly that we should greet one another with holy kisses (Romans 16:16, 1 Corinthians 16:20, 2 Corinthians

13:12, 1 Thessalonians 5:26). Far be it from me to forbid that which God commands.

The impression I get from the scriptures is that kissing can be a way to:

- say "hello" (Genesis 29:11)
- say "goodbye" (Genesis 31:28)
- bless (1 Sam 10:1)
- worship (Psalm 2:12 ESV, Luke 7:38)
- show brotherly love (1 Samuel 20:41 ESV, 1 Peter 5:14)
- show sexual desire (Song of Songs 7:9)

Which led me to ask myself, *Could it be that when we forbid kissing, we make it only a sexual act?*

What would the Church look like if we embraced kissing? I suspect it would be a bit awkward at first for Americans. Our culture seems to be walking away from kissing. TV and movies show fewer kisses these days and instead cut straight to the bedroom or to the next scene.

I do realize that there's a difference between kissing and *kissing.* So I hear you asking, "At which point does a kiss cease to be a holy kiss?"

My answer is that I think you're asking the wrong person.

As with a lot of the specifics of dating, we have to let the Holy Spirit guide us. God gives us a lot more freedom than the Purity Police would have you believe. For some, eating meat may be a sin, while for others it isn't (1 Corinthians 8). I think this "meat principle" applies to a lot of areas of life.

> Far be it from me to forbid that which God commands.

The primary commandment that God gives us for our interactions with other people is that we love them as much as we love ourselves (Mark 12:31). Jesus tells us to do unto others as we would have them do unto us (Luke 6:31).

As we seek God on whether it's okay with Him if we kiss, we need to keep in mind the commandment that we love one another. It's also a good idea to seek God as a couple and make the decision together before you end up in the heat of the moment.

> Seek God as a couple and make the decision together before you end up in the heat of the moment.

Loving someone means not pressuring them into violating their conscience. Those with the stronger conscience should support those with the weaker conscience. If one person has the faith to kiss without it violating their conscience but the other one doesn't, then they should not kiss. To do otherwise would be unloving.

If the Holy Spirit is in your heart, He'll guide you. If not, rules won't make a difference one way or the other.

Sincerely,

Thomas

Question #10: Are you saying that if I use Traditional Dating, I'll have a long and happy marriage like your grandparents?

Mr. Thomas,

My parents are divorced and most of my friends' parents are divorced as well. I would rather be single than go through a divorce. Will Traditional Dating guarantee that I will have a happy marriage like your grandparents?

Discouraged,
O

Dear O,

No system is perfect. As the book of Job shows us, sometimes bad things happen to good people, and good things happen to bad people. We're all broken, and any human system will contain that brokenness. Some systems are more broken than others. Place your trust in Christ, not in the system you're using.

But just because no relationship system is perfect doesn't mean you should avoid all systems. Cookies can burn in any recipe, but that's no excuse to reject the idea of recipes altogether. The better the recipe you're working from, the better your chance for success.

The best things in life require risk. You are not doomed to repeat the mistakes of your parents. Contrary to what the media says, most marriages are happy and the majority of them last a lifetime. You can have a happy marriage!

Praying for you,

Thomas

Question #11: How do I say no to a second date without sounding mean or sending the wrong message?

Thomas,

I went on a date with J and while we had a good time, I don't think we're a good fit. Don't get me wrong. I think J is a great guy. I just don't think he is a great guy for me. He has asked me out for a second date and I don't really want to go. I know that guys can take rejection really hard and I don't want to break his heart.

What should I do?

C

Dear C,

One of the reasons Modern Courtship appeals to some women is that they don't have to say no to young men who ask them out. In Traditional Dating, however, saying no is important both for you and for the guy who wants a second date.

If saying no is generally difficult for you, I recommend you read *The Power of a Positive No* by William Ury. That book is packed with useful advice that will help you in many areas of your life.

Here are five tips on how to say no in a way that is both firm and kind.

Tip #1: Be Honest

Some women will keep going out with a man in an attempt to keep from hurting his feelings. This is self-defeating because they're avoiding a smaller pain now for what will be a bigger pain later. Don't deceive someone into thinking you're more interested than you are. Staying in a futureless relationship delays you from finding a husband and keeps him from finding a wife.

Tip #2: Affirm

Just because you aren't a good match doesn't mean that he's a bad person. Tell him what you admire about him. Consider something like, "John, I admire your heart for the Lord and what a hard worker you are. I just don't think we are a good match."

Tip #3: Be Clear

This is *not* the time to send mixed signals. Don't say that you're busy that night. That's code for "ask me again some other time." Being clear doesn't mean you need to tell him everything that's wrong with him. He just needs to know not to ask you out again.

Tip #4: Don't Blame God

Some Christian young women say things like, "God told me not to go out with you." This seems easy because you're not rejecting him. God is.

Imagine the effect on a young man's psyche as woman after woman blames God for why he can't ask them out on

#CourtshipInCrisis

a date. He'll get the impression that God is angry with him when in reality the young women are just afraid to tell him no.

This kind of rejection is unclear. He's wondering if you actually like him, but it's God who is saying no. That leads to questions about whether God will change His mind later. Better to be direct and take ownership of your decision so there's no ongoing confusion for either of you.

Tip #5: Have a Bigger Yes in Mind

In *The Power of a Positive No*, William Ury points out that the key to giving a positive no is to have a bigger yes that you're affirming in your mind. The best rejection I ever received followed this principle.

The young woman said, "Thomas, there is a woman out there who is a better match for you than I am." That was honest (I hope!). It affirmed me, making me feel that I wasn't worthless and unworthy of anyone. It was clear and left no doubt as to whether I had a chance with her. She didn't blame God for her decision. Perhaps God had told her not to go out with me, but she didn't use that as her reason for saying no.

Feel free to adopt her line as your own. I don't think she would mind.

Bonus Tip: Recommend a Friend

If he's a great guy in general and just a bad match for you, consider connecting him with a friend of yours who might be a better match. This sort of referring to a friend used to happen all the time in old-school Traditional Dating, and it's how a lot of folks met their match. This will also help you shift your mindset away from Modern Courtship and Modern Dating, both of which result in lingering claims on someone you don't intend to marry.

Recommending a friend also takes the bite out of the rejection. It's one thing to say he's a great guy. It's another thing to introduce him to a friend.

Blessings,

Thomas

Question #12: Are double dates a good idea?

Dear Thomas,

I want to start traditional dating, but I'm nervous. What do you think about getting my feet wet and going on a few double dates to start?

Sincerely,
V

Dear V,

I am a big fan of double dates. The benefits of couples-based group activities are as follows:

Benefit #1: You're Less Likely to Get Stuck in the "Friendzone"

Gus and Sally are friends. They're part of a group of friends who regularly meet to "hang out" and to participate in group activities. As they become closer friends, Gus sees them as just friends while Sally has secretly started trying on wedding dresses in her mind.

Gus has no idea that Sally is thinking of the relationship as something more. Gus, who rarely thinks about the relationship, thinks it is cruising along nicely on the highway of friendship. But for Sally, the relationship has become a cul-de-sac of broken dreams. The faster things move for her, the more likely everything is to topple over.

This is such a common occurrence that my generation now has a word for it. We'd say that Sally is stuck in the "friendzone." She's hoping for romance, but all she has is a friendship. The friendzone is an unfortunate and inevitable side effect of group dating.

It's fine to be friends before being romantically interested in someone, but it's also possible for friendship to become an end rather than a means. Too much of a good thing can become a bad thing. This is like putting so many sticks on a fire that you smother it.

Traditional Dating is more intentional than the group dating elements of Modern Dating and Modern Courtship.

Benefit #2: Double Dating Gives You a Good Idea of What You're Looking for and What You're Not Looking For

Being "a couple" for one meal gives you a data point on that person's personality. It's a fun way to get to know how their personality interacts with those of your friends. A group of four friends is a safe place to experience "coupleness" without all the pressure of going steady. All of this data leads to better decisions.

Benefit #3: Couples-Based Group Events Force Men to Give Women Specific Attention

Lots of amazing girls out there aren't getting asked out, because they never get specific attention. They disappear into the group unnoticed and unpursued. If the guys in their community would spend time with them one-on-one, they'd discover how amazing the girls are, instead of thinking of them as So-and-So of *Teen Girl Squad*.

When these girls' interactions with guys are limited to only group settings, it's easy for them to blend into the wallpaper. And yes, this can happen to quiet guys as easily as it happens to quiet girls.

Benefit #4: Double Dating Keeps Things Fun & Casual

The Modern Courtship movement turned "casual" into a dirty word, and to the degree that they reject "casual sex," they're right to do so. But just like blowing too hard can extinguish a small fire, too much intensity too soon can kill a relationship. During the early stages of a fire, you have to protect it from intense wind—the same wind that would cause a more mature fire to grow even hotter.

Intensity can also lead to heartbreak and "giving your heart away" to someone you don't know well. The way my grandmother's generation protected their hearts was by keeping the relationship casual while they were getting to know someone.

> Modern Courtship traded casual for intense and traded fun for awkward. It's time to redeem casual relationships.

A double date also reduces the likelihood of word vomit,where people divulge their deepest feelings, deepest wounds, and past relationships on their first date. That's too much too soon. Double-dating encourages couples to slow down.

Modern Courtship traded casual for intense and traded fun for awkward. It's time to redeem casual relationships.

Sincerely,

Thomas

Question #13: Should I avoid women who say, 'Talk to my dad'?

Dear Thomas,

I'm interested in a woman who is the only daughter of a protective and courtship-minded man. He firmly believes that any man who wants to date his daughter should have his explicit permission. I asked her out to coffee and she told me I had to talk to her dad first. Should I pursue her, or is this a recipe for disaster?

Unsure,

K

Dear K,

One reason I wrote "Why Courtship is Fundamentally Flawed" is because about half a dozen godly, single men asked me to write it. They did their best to honor God through courtship and had ended up with broken spirits. The last thing I want for you is a broken spirit.

I'm not saying it's wrong to pursue a girl who requires a man to fight a dragon before winning her heart. But if you were a friend of mine, I'd advise against it in most situations for the following reasons:

7 Reasons I Don't Recommend Going After Dragon-Guarded Women

1. **Getting parental approval at the start makes the relationship too intense too quickly.** Getting permission to enter a relationship whose purpose is marriage, before getting to know the girl, is like stepping on the gas while also stepping on the brakes. It's not a healthy way to start a relationship. Better to begin as "just friends" who get coffee or ice cream every now and again. See Chapter 4 for all of the problems that come from getting too intense too soon.

2. **There's a good chance that "talk to my dad" is really her way of saying no.** Women sometimes feel bad about hurting a guy's feelings by saying no. It's easier for them to send the man to her dad who can say no for her. Does that make it right? No. But that's the unfortunate reality of some situations. So my advice is to take the hint and accept "talk to my dad" for the no that it really is.

3. **There may be maturity issues.** If she doesn't feel mature enough to give you a direct answer, there's a chance she's not mature enough for the relationship. The kinds of girls protected by Dragon Fathers are often the kind of girls who don't have a lot of freedom to make their own choices, and that can stunt their emotional maturity. They may still live at home and lack the real-world experience for the kind of serious, marriage-bound courtship the dad will likely insist you have.

4. **There may be trust issues.** Assuming she's an adult (at least eighteen), the fact that her parents don't let her make this decision reveals their distrust. If her parents, who have known her all her life, don't trust her, then why should you? Yes, she could be an amazing, trustworthy girl whose suspicious parents are unwilling to cede control to her. On the other hand, these trust issues may instead be a symptom of her lack of trust in God. You have to decide if that's something you're willing to confront (along with her Dragon Father). You might be stepping on a landmine with this relationship.

5. **The parents may need to be "handled" for the rest of the relationship.** Some of the comments on my "Why Courtship is Fundamentally Flawed" blog post say that the man should "man up" and "handle" the father. This can put an undue strain on the relationship and can lead to some very sad outcomes. Ideally, family gatherings should be something couples look forward to. No one wants Christmas to be a war zone.

6. **It makes the relationship mathematically more complex.** Two people make one relationship. Three people triples the number of relationships to three. A true

courtship with all four parents involved amounts to fifteen different relationships. Any of these relationships can add tension to the romantic relationship. The more people in a relationship, the harder it is to "~~kiss~~ side-hug and make up." The inevitable reconciliation needed for a healthy relationship can become nearly impossible. The less-flawed model is to have only one relationship between two people who get advice from four trusted advisors.

7. **It's not your place to change someone's family.** Unconditional love means you love without conditions. This means accepting someone for who they are. Going into a relationship with a goal to change someone or their family isn't love. At best, it's foolishness, and at worst, it's manipulation. This goes both ways.

I admit there can be great rewards for the knight who fights off the dragon to win the hand of the princess. This is an old story, and one knight may succeed where many others have fallen.

I've heard many stories of married women who are thankful for their dragon-fighting husbands, but there is nothing new under the sun. Domineering fathers will always be with us. I agree that it's unfair to doom adult daughters to life-long singleness.

But my advice is to find a girl without a dragon flying around her castle. Relationships are hard enough already without having to avoid getting burned to a crisp in the process.

Sincerely,

Thomas

Question #14: How Do I Switch to a Traditional Dating Mindset?

Hey Thomas,

I'm a twenty-eight-year-old man, and I grew up with Modern Courtship my whole life. So far, none of my six siblings have gotten married, and we all want to try Traditional Dating. But thinking that dating is "okay" is a long way from actually doing it. Any advice on how we can adopt a Traditional Dating mindset in real life?

Trying to change,

A

Dear A,

The best way change your mindset is to first change your actions. Start asking girls on dates. Believe it or not, most single women want to be asked out on a date. This is especially true if they know you practice Traditional Dating and you have honorable intentions.

Talk with your brothers and hold one another accountable to ask a certain number of women out on dates each month. The more you do it, the more you'll overcome your fear, and the easier it will become.

Encourage your sisters to say yes to first dates from

strangers. They can drive to a neutral location and meet him there if they don't know him well. That way they can leave if things get awkward while still giving the guy a chance. Once word goes out in a community that a woman says yes to first dates, the dates will keep coming. The easier they are to ask, the more men will ask them out.

Sincerely,

Thomas

Question #15: I want to try Traditional Dating, but all of my friends are courtship-minded. What should I do?

Thomas,

It seems I'm kind of stuck. In the area where I live and in the circles in which I roll, all of my friends practice Modern Courtship. I'm a bit discouraged, because I'm not the most social person and these friends are pretty much all I've got.

Do you have any suggestions on what I can do about this? Anything I could try to better my situation?

Discouraged,

Z

Hi Z,

I feel you. The challenge with shifting away from Modern Courtship is that you can't do it on your own. The more people who practice Traditional Dating, the easier it is for everyone. Part of the reason I wrote this book was to help make finding love easier for people like you.

Here are a few options for you to consider:

Option #1: Convince Your Friends to Try Traditional Dating

I suspect many of your friends are as frustrated as you are. They want to get married too, but they feel stuck. The first thing you could try is to encourage them to read this book or at least the blog post "Why Courtship is Fundamentally Flawed".

Consider giving a copy of this book to your pastor, and see if he'll recommend Traditional Dating from the pulpit. Why am I suggesting this? Modern Courtship has been preached so passionately that many people feel they need permission from their pastor to try Traditional Dating.

Another thing to try is to loan this book to a friend. The intent of this book is to convince readers that Traditional Dating is a tried-and-true method of creating and inspiring romantic relationships that lead to more marriages than Modern Courtship. If you're convinced, perhaps your friends will agree as well. You can find more resources about Traditional Dating at www.ThomasUmstattd.com.

Option #2: Get a New Group of Friends

I can't tell you how many people I've talked to who found their husband or wife after moving to a new church. Some churches have a dismal dating culture where everyone is stuck in singleness. If you can't change the culture, perhaps you can find a healthier culture elsewhere. You can always come back to your church once you're married.

Option #3: Try Online Dating

Another thing you can do is to sign up for an online match-making site. These days, one out of three married couples meet online.[1] I know it may seem strange to see a recommendation to try online dating in a Traditional Dating book, but matchmaking is a key component of this traditional model.

People have been using computers to help them find matches since before the Internet. They used to mail in paper questionnaires to buildings where the computer filled an entire floor and ran on punch cards.

Sincerely,

Thomas

11

A LETTER TO THE READER

Dear Reader,

Thank you for hearing me out and for reading the whole book. I hope you enjoyed it.

As you consider giving Traditional Dating a try, I hope you find that it's a simple, fun, and ethical way to find a great match. The more people who try Traditional Dating, the easier it will be for everyone.

Traditional Dating has helped countless people find the love of their lives. Who knows? Perhaps we could even see culture shift away from the hookup-and-breakup pain of Modern Dating and the loneliness of Modern Courtship.

Ideas can change the world if they can spread. The fastest way to spread an idea is to talk about it on social media. Consider sharing some of the callouts in this book on Facebook or Twitter. You can also join the conversation about this book online by using the #CourtshipInCrisis hashtag on your social network of choice. You can find copy-and-paste versions of the Tweetables at http://www.CourtshipInCrisis.com/tweetables.

If you're a single woman, talking about Traditional Dating on social media signals to the men around you that they can ask you out without you perceiving it as a marriage proposal. This makes it a lot easier for them to ask you out, and you will get asked out on more dates.

The same goes for single men. As you talk about Traditional Dating online, women will find it easier to say yes to a date with you since they won't need to mentally try on wedding dresses first.

After my blog post "Why Courtship is Fundamentally Flawed" spread on Facebook, I heard from singles who were going out on dates for the first time. This really does work!

Consider giving this book to your pastor or sharing it with a friend.

I am available for speaking engagements at churches, youth groups, schools, and homeschool events. For more information about booking me to speak, visit www.ThomasUmstattd.com/speaking.

If you want to find other people who practice Traditional Dating through an online matchmaking service, just put #TraditionalDating in your profile. I would love to hear from you!

You can find me at:

- **Website:** www.CourtshipInCrisis.com
- **Facebook:** www.facebook.com/ThomasUmstattd
- **Twitter**: @ThomasUmstattd
- **Email**: courtshipincrisis@thomasumstattd.com
- **Snail Mail**: P.O Box 5690 Austin, TX 78763

My hope is that Traditional Dating will help you find the love of your life and help end the Courtship Crisis.

Sincerely,

Thomas Umstattd Jr.

PART 4

APPENDIX

CREDITS

Manuscript Developer & Book Coach

Erin MacPherson

Lead Editor

Ben Wolf

Copy Editor

Frank Ball

Proofreader

Lindsay Franklin

Cover Design

Zubimarva Setiawan

Interior Page Design

Margaret Stroud

Back Cover Design

Ashley Mays

Alpha Readers

Martha Artyomenko
Mary DeMuth
Tim Gilmour
Geno Hildebrandt
Abigail Maxwell
Margaret Stroud
Ginger Umstattd
Tom Umstattd

Research Team

Tim Gilmour
Hans Jensen
Abigail Maxwell
MaryKate Parker
Margaret Stroud

Launch Team

Christopher Arnold
David C. & Pamela Black
Nadine Brandes
Joie Brannan
Virginia Brannan
James Cain
Mr & Mrs Barton & Christina Durbin
Bernice Gaona
James Y. Gochnauer
Rosemary Graber
David Hanson
Elizabeth Harris

Katie Hart
Andrea Hayes
Jason & Jacqueline Isaacs
Edward Jaax
Erin Larkin
Abigail Maxwell
Stephen McCants
Faber McMullen III
Madelaine & Jim Morris
Erin Schlomach
Bryan Shufelt
McKenzie Taylor
Johnathan Taylor
Tony Tovar
Cynthia Umstattd
Ginger Umstattd
Tom Umstattd, CPA
Adam Weisenburger
Andrew C. White

THANKS

To my parents, Tom & Ginger Umstattd, for your prayers, support, and countless hours helping me edit this manuscript. Thank you for standing with me even when the criticisms on Facebook were making you cry.

To my siblings Cynthia, David, William, and John for your encouragement and support.

My grandparents for talking sense to a young man even when he was not willing to listen.

To the Castle Media Group team for working hard for a boss who was spending more time on his book than on his company.

To the people who backed this book on Kickstarter. This book would not exist without you.

Martha Artyomenko, Erin MacPherson, and Kathi Lipp—thank you for convincing me to write this book. You helped push me to take the book from idea to reality.

To everyone who shared their stories.

Amanda Dewoody for helping keep me organized, on task, and on time. Your encouragement cut two months off the time to make this book.

Thunderbird Coffee for keeping me caffeinated and for providing a low-pressure place for first dates.

Mary DeMuth, James L. Rubart, Tony Tovar, Erin MacPherson, James Scott Bell, Randy Ingermanson, Kathi Lipp, Lacy Williams, Nicole O'Dell, Tricia Goyer, and Susan May Warren—thank you for encouraging me as I worked on this book and for helping me navigate the publishing process.

Debra Fileta for writing the foreword and for writing about dating on www.TrueLoveDates.com before it was cool to talk about dating.

Tim Stewart for challenging my ideas and keeping me on my feet.

Pastor Geno Hildebrandt and the entire family at Hope Chapel. Your encouragement and support means more than you know. Thank you for making Hope Chapel a safe place for hurting people.

Jesus for saving me and giving me hope.

About the Author

Thomas Umstattd Jr. is the former head of Practical-Courtship.com and co-founder of the Austin Rhetoric Club, a homeschool speech and debate club in Austin, Texas. He is an international speaker and CEO of Castle Media Group, LLC. Thomas sits on the board of directors for several nonprofits, including Texas Alliance for Life.

ENDNOTES

Introduction

1. *The Dave Ramsey Show*. Narrated by Dave Ramsey. Produced by Blake Thompson. The Lampo Group, Inc.

Chapter 1

1. Wendy Wang and Kim Parker, "Record Share of Americans Have Never Married," *Pew Research Center*, September 24, 2014, http://www.pewsocialtrends.org/2014/09/24/record-share-of-americans-have-never-married/ (accessed June 20, 2015).
2. U.S. Department of Health, Education, and Welfare, Public Health Service. Health Resources Administration, National Center for Health Statistics, *Division of Vital Statistics*, "100 Years of Marriage and Divorce Statistics United States, 1867-1967," by Alexander A. Plateris, Ph.D, DHEW (HRA) 74-1902. Washington, D.C.: U.S.: U.S. Government Printing Office, 1973, http://www.cdc.gov/nchs/data/series/sr_21/sr21_024.pdf (accessed June 20, 2015).

3. Ibid, 28.

4. Sabrina Tavernise, "Married Couples are No Longer a Majority, Study Finds," *The New York Times*, May 26, 2011, http://www.nytimes.com/2011/05/26/us/26marry.html?_r=1 (accessed June 20, 2015).

5. D'Vera Cohn, Jeffrey S. Passel, Wendy Wang, and Gretchen Livingston, "Barely Half of U.S. Adults are Married—A Record Low," Pew Research Center, Washington, D.C. (December 14, 2011), http://www.pewsocialtrends.org/files/2011/12/Marriage-Decline.pdf (accessed June 20, 2015).

6. Wang and Parker, "Record Share of Americans Have Never Married," *Pew Research Center*, September 24, 2014, http://www.pewsocialtrends.org/2014/09/24/record-share-of-americans-have-never-married/

7. Aristotle, *Politics*, 1.2, trans.Benjamin Jowett.

8. "Family Structure and Children's Education," *FamilyFacts.org.* http://www.familyfacts.org/briefs/35/family-structure-and-childrens-education (accessed June 17, 2015).

9. Patrick Fagan, Robert Rector, Kirk Johnson, and America Peterson. "The Positive Effects of Marriage: A Book of Charts," *The Heritage Foundation*, Washington, D.C. (2002). http://thf_media.s3.amazonaws.com/2002/pdf/positive_effects_of_marriage.pdf (accessed June 20, 2015).

10. "Marriage and Family as Deterrents from Delinquency, Violence and Crime," *FamilyFacts.org.* http://www.familyfacts.org/briefs/26/marriage-and-family-as-deterrents-from-delinquency-violence-and-crime (accessed June 17, 2015).

11. Patrick Fagan et al., "The Positive Effects," 13.

12. Gretchen Livingston, "Less than half of U.S. kids today live in a 'traditional' family," *Pew Research Center*, December 22, 2014, http://www.pewresearch.org/fact-tank/2014/12/22/less-than-half-of-u-s-kids-today-live-in-a-traditional-family/ (accessed June 20, 2015).

13. "There really is such a thing as wedded bliss: Married couples are happier than singles says new study following benefits of matrimony," *DailyMail.com*, January 10, 2015, http://www.dailymail.co.uk/news/article-2904986/There-really-thing-wedded-bliss-Married-couples-happier-singles-says-new-study-following-benefits-matrimony.html (accessed June 20, 2015).

14. "Study: Married Couples Live Longer, Healthier Lives Than Singles," *CBS Cleveland*, November 14, 2012, http://cleveland.cbslocal.com/2012/11/14/study-married-couples-live-longer-healthier-lives-than-singles/.

15. Associated Press, "Study: Married folks have fewer heart problems," *USA Today*, March 28, 2014, http://www.usatoday.com/story/news/nation/2014/03/28/married-fewer-heart-problems/7017461/ (accessed June 20, 2015).

16. Cari Nierenberg, "Married People More Likely To Survive Cancer," *WebMD*, October 14, 2011, http://www.webmd.com/cancer/news/20111014/married-people-more-likely-survive-cancer (accessed June 20, 2015).

17. Jenny Hope, "How being married can cut your risk of Alzheimer's in later life," *DailyMail.com*, July 2, 2009, http://www.dailymail.co.uk/health/article-1197191/How-married-cut-risk-Alzheimers-later-life.html (accessed June 20, 2015).

18. "The Benefits of Marriage," *FamilyFacts.org*. http://www.familyfacts.org/briefs/1/the-benefits-of-marriage (accessed June 18, 2015).

19. "The Benefits of Marriage," *FamilyFacts.org*.

Chapter 2

1. Titus Livius, *The History of Rome, Vol. 1*, trans. Rev. Canon Roberts, ed. Ernest Rhys (London: J.M. Dent & Sons, Ltd., 1905), http://mcadams.posc.mu.edu/txt/ah/Livy/Livy01.html (accessed June 20, 2015).
2. John Locke, *The Two Treatises of Civil Government* (1689), Online Library of Liberty, http://oll.libertyfund.org/titles/222 (accessed June 18, 2015).
3. Ellen Rothman, *Hands and Hearts: A History of Courtship in America*, (New York: Basic Books Incorporated, 1984), 28.
4. Ibid, 25.
5. Ibid, 27.
6. Inquirer Wire Services, "Study: Unwed Sex Common In Late 1700s," *Philly.com*, August 30, 1988, http://articles.philly.com/1988-08-30/news/26256681_1_pregnancy-marriage-courtship (accessed June 20, 2015).
7. Rothman, *A History of Courtship in America*, 138
8. Inquirer Wire Services, "Study: Unwed Sex Common in Late 1700s."
9. Beth L. Bailey, *From Front Porch to Back Seat*, (Baltimore: Johns Hopkins University Press, 1988).
10. Richard Mullendore, quoted in Lee Shearer, "University vice president addresses area businessmen," *Athens Banner-Herald*, August 1, 2003, http://onlineathens.com/stories/080103/uga_20030801045.shtml
11. Nolan Feeney, "Violent Crime Drops to Lowest Level Since 1978," *Time*, November 10, 2014, http://time.com/3577026/crime-rates-drop-1970s/ (accessed June 20, 2015).
12. Rothman, *A History of Courtship in America*, 139.

Chapter 3

1. Wikipedia contributors, "Sexual revolution," *Wikipedia, The Free Encyclopedia,* https://en.wikipedia.org/w/index.php?title=Sexual_revolution&oldid=665371900 (accessed June 18, 2015).
2. Gary Langer, "Poll: American Sex Survey," *ABCNews. com,* October 21, 2004, https://abcnews.go.com/images/Politics/959a1AmericanSexSurvey.pdf (accessed June 20, 2015).
3. Michael Kosfeld, Markus Heinrichs, Paul J. Zak, Urs Fischbacher, & Ernst Fehr, "Oxytocin increases trust in humans," Nature 435 (2 June 2005): 673-676, doi 10.1038/nature03701, http://www.nature.com/nature/journal/v435/n7042/abs/nature03701.html (accessed June 18, 2015).
4. Shira Yufe, "'Love Hormone' Oxytocin Linked To Domestic Violence," *The Trauma & Mental Health Report,* June 6, 2014, http://trauma.blog.yorku.ca/2014/06/love-hormone-oxytocin-linked-to-domestic-violence/ (accessed June 20, 2015).
5. Scott M. Stanley, Galena Kline Rhoades, and Howard J. Markman, "Sliding Versus Deciding: Inertia and the Premarital Cohabitation Effect," *Family Relations* 55 (2006): 499–509, https://public.psych.iastate.edu/ccutrona/psych592a/articles/Sliding%20and%20cohabitation.pdf, (accessed June 20, 2015).

Chapter 4

1. "True Love Doesn't Wait. Really!" *True Love Doesn't Wait,* http://truelovedoesntwait.com/ (accessed June 20, 2015).

2. David Crank, "Approaches to Courtship / Betrothal: The Differing Teachings on Courtship & Betrothal," Unless the Lord 4.2 (2003), http://www.unlessthelordmagazine. com/articles/Courtship%20Approaches.htm (accessed June 20, 2015).
3. Wikipedia contributors "Courtship Display," *Wikipedia, the Free Encyclopedia*, https://en.wikipedia.org/wiki/ Courtship_display (accessed June 20, 2015).
4. Douglas Wilson, *Her Hand in Marriage* (Moscow, ID: Canon Press, 1997), 15.
5. Ibid., 24.
6. Ibid., 22.
7. This is a quote from *The Princess Bride.*

Chapter 6

1. Roy F. Baumeister and John Tierney. *Willpower: Rediscovering the Greatest Human Strength.* (New York: The Penguin Press, 2011), 22.

Chapter 8

1. Shaunti Feldhahn. *The Good News About Marriage,* (Multnomah Books, 2014).

Chapter 9

1. This quote is usually attributed to C.S. Lewis but we could not find evidence of that. It may be from Rick Warren.
2. J.R.R. Tolkien, The Fellowship of the Ring (New York: Houghton Mifflin Harcourt Publishing Company, 1994) 322.

Chapter 10

1. AFP RelaxNews, "One-third of married couples in U.S. meet online: study," *Daily News*, June 4, 2013, http://www.nydailynews.com/life-style/one-third-u-s-marriages-start-online-dating-study-article-1.1362743

Made in the USA
Las Vegas, NV
24 October 2023

79623745R00127